PUEBLOS

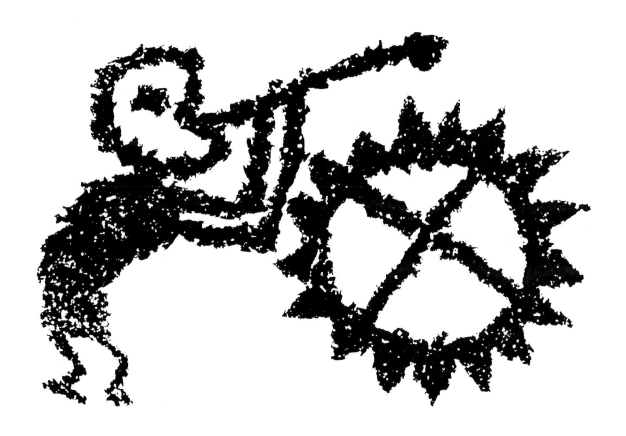

PUEBLOS

Copyright by U. Bär Verlag, Zurich (Switzerland) 1989; original title: DIE PUEBLOS

Translation copyright © 1990 by Facts On File, Inc.

Facts On File, Inc.
460 Park Avenue South
New York NY 10016
USA

Facts On File Limited
Collins Street
Oxford OX4 1XJ
NSW 2113
United Kingdom

Library of Congress Cataloging-in-Publication Data
Acatos, Sylvio.
    [Pueblos. English]
    Pueblos / Sylvio Acatos [text] ; Maximilien Bruggmann [photography].
        p.   cm.
    Translation of: Die Pueblos.
    Includes bibliographical references.
    ISBN 0-8160-2437-5
    1. Pueblo Indians—Antiquities.   2. Southwest, New—Antiquities.
    I. Bruggmann, Maximilien.   II. Title.
E99.P9A2313   1990
979'.01—dc20   89-49601

A British CIP catalogue record for this book is available from the British Library.

Facts On File books are available at special discounts when purchased in bulk quantities for businesses, associations, institutions or sales promotions. Please call our Special Sales Department in New York at 212/683-2244 (dial 800/322-8755 except in NY, AK or HI) or in Oxford at 865/7283999.

Composition by Facts On File, Inc.
Manufactured by Trilogy
Printed in Italy

10 9 8 7 6 5 4 3 2 1

For abbreviations used in the captions, see page 240: Abbreviations.

Jacket: Sea shell pendant, the convex surface of which is set with more than 340 turquoise pieces with a single red shell piece set in the center. Diameter: 3.64 inches. Mogollon Culture, ASM.

Endpaper: A typical design used to decorate Anasazi baskets. It is based on the artful repetition of a triangle in positive and negative play.

Page 1: Incising: Kokopelli, the flute player, with the sun symbol. This figure is often found among the petroglyphs of the Southwest. Length: 14 inches. Galisteo (New Mexico).

Pages 2–3: Mimbres pot with a stylized scorpion within a circle of round and zig-zag lines and a hole in the middle. The pot was "killed" in the grave of the owner, so that the spirit of the pot and that of the deceased may meet again in the hereafter. Diameter: 9.2–10.8 inches. From the collection of E.H. Morris, UCM.

Pages 4–5: Newspaper Rock: Combination of animals, hand and footprints, as well as figures representing people, shields, spirals and sun symbols. The pictographs span several centuries and are therefore difficult to date. The wall is 16 feet high. The large "wheel" represents a decorated shield; the largest figure in the upper right hand corner is 14 inches tall. Newspaper Rock State Historical Monument, Indian Creek State Park (Utah).

Pages 6–7: Spruce Tree House, one of the most impressive and best preserved Pueblo towns in Mesa Verde National Park (Colorado). In the foreground, a ladder leads into the subterranean *kiva*, the round ceremonial chamber. The pueblo was inhabited from about 1200 to 1300. Anasazi Culture.

Page 10: A split twig figure of a deer made of delicate willow branches. The shape is highly stylized and very expressionistic, and is a fine example of the use made of the simplest material. Height: 2.6 inches, Walnut Canyon (Arizona), Western Archaic Period, 2000-1000 B.C., MNA.

Page 12: Typical geometric design used on Chaco Canyon pottery (New Mexico). The triangle may symbolize lightning.

MAXIMILIEN BRUGGMANN

PHOTOGRAPHS

SYLVIO ACATOS

TEXT

TRANSLATED BY
BARBARA FRITZEMEIER

WOLFGANG LINDIG

FOREWORD

PUEBLOS

PREHISTORIC INDIAN CULTURES OF THE SOUTHWEST

☑ Facts On File
New York • Oxford

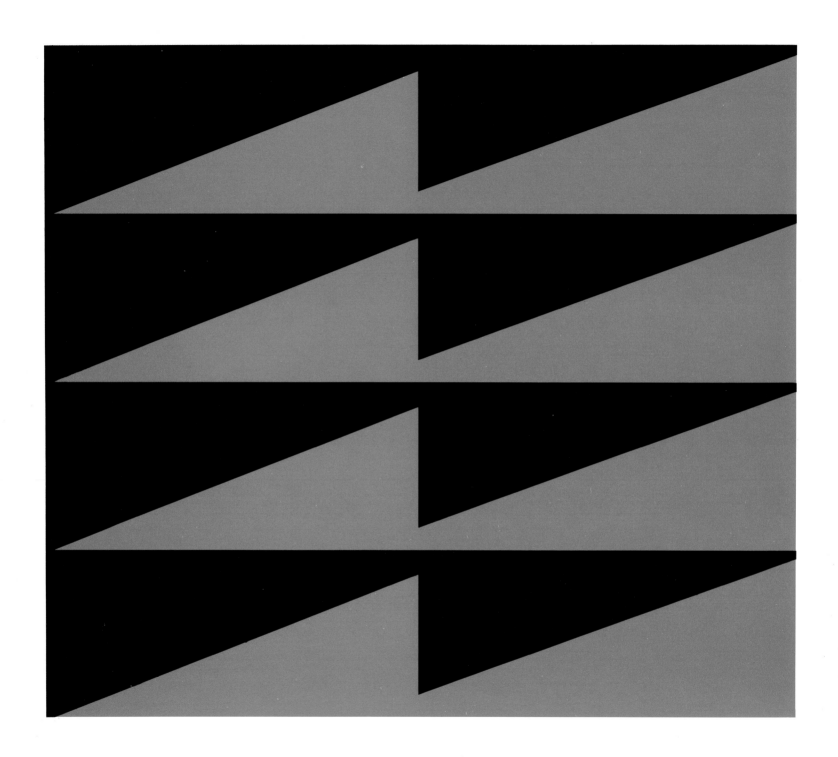

FOREWORD

The North American Southwest is a unique world, marked by the traces of its Indian past. Unlike other parts of North America, this arid landscape has preserved many aspects of Indian life that date back centuries. In addition, the indigenous culture has been influenced by the incursion of the great Meso-American peoples to the south. The Southwest is therefore also on the periphery of the ancient Mexican cultures with their rich diversity. Within the ambit of their highly cultured neighbors, the Indian peoples who have lived in the Southwest for the last two millennia, inspired by the magnificent landscape surrounding them, have independently produced a distinctive culture well worth the respect of later Americans and Europeans, who are so proud of their own past.

In view of their prehistoric cultural heritage and the unchanged, imposing land in which they lived, it is clear that the historic Indian people who inhabited this land sought the source of their creation and became one with nature, which fed, clothed and sheltered them. This is also true—and is in fact especially obvious—in the case of the Athapaskans, particularly the Navajo, people who migrated to the Southwest only a few centuries ago. In their lives they seek harmony with the elements of the universe, and only in finding this precarious equilibrium can they experience the meaning of life. This longing for universal harmony takes form in the rich ceremonial life of these people, which is unique among North American Indians.

The considerable bond that the Navajo have with their homeland on one hand reflects the grandeur and beauty of the land, and on the other indicates their interconnection with the traditions of the land's ancient inhabitants, the Pueblos. An unbroken self-image, paired with a belief in the power and ultimate significance of their concept of the world, is what the modern Pueblo Indians derive from their ancestors.

Numerous books, many of them richly illustrated, are available to introduce us to Southwest Indian archaeology. Most are works by scholars and provide the reader with extensive information about a complex cultural history. There are also illustrated volumes known only to a small group of enthusiasts who have fallen victim to the "lure of the West." This volume is entirely new in its approach. The photographs are by a master of the art, the text by a cultural historian who interprets the history of the Indian people, so extensively preserved here in the Southwest, as part of a creative energy that is universally human, a central theme, which runs throughout the text.

Professor Dr. Wolfgang Lindig
Institut für Historische Ethnologie der Universität Frankfurt/Main
(Institute for Historical Ethnology of the University of Frankfurt/Main)

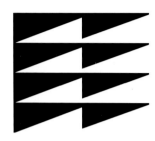 THE UNIVERSAL

A discussion of the North American Indians often brings to mind an image of the red-skinned people native to the vast, dry plains of the American West or the dark, dense forests of the Atlantic regions. This red-skinned warrior was immortalized in the novels of James Fenimore Cooper (1789–1851), which depict the heroic conflict between Indians and white pioneers in *The Last of the Mohicans* (1826), *The Prairie* (1827), and other works. And he was depicted in the paintings of Karl Bodmer, the Swiss artist who accompanied Prince Maximilian of Wied on an expedition up the Missouri in the 1830s, and George Catlin (1796–1872), whose painstakingly accurate sketches and watercolor paintings are frequently primary source materials for ethnologists and historians. The Indian also appeared on the movie screen in films by the director John Huston and others.

The Indian heroes of James Fenimore Cooper's works, however, are only storybook figures. They are appealing and fascinating, but have no basis in ethnographic reality. One of the great authorities on Native American cultures, Clark Wissler, has pointed out that nearly all depictions of Indians, whether idealized or negatively distorted, bear little resemblance to reality: "…the picture is a composite, welded together partly under white influence, and the reader now knows that this picture presents a generalized Indian, rather than the reality. If one had walked through the United States about 1600, he would have noted ever-changing styles of clothing, housing and standards of living. Speech, too, would have been different at every village or camp."

At the time when the first Europeans set foot on the North American continent, approximately three million native people lived in an area extending from Alaska to the Gulf of Mexico and from the Atlantic to the Pacific Oceans. Today, differentiation and regionalization are fashionable; concepts such as universality and communality are not considered acceptable. People want to believe exclusively in the individual. This trend has influenced most of Western thought for the past 20 years. In his book *Beyond Culture* (1976) anthropologist Edward T. Hall, who specializes in intercultural relationships and the problems encountered in communication across cultural barriers, uses the example of a student who observed at least fifteen differences in the ways Indians and non-Indians walk.

It is true that the various native American cultures are fundamentally very different, but in the end there are also similarities. One must be willing to see the common aspects while resisting the impulse to think of these cultures as one. There have always been two divergent views of human history, or, more accurately, the histories of the different peoples

Pages 14-15: Petroglyphs in red ochre nicknamed "Supernova"—a 10-pointed star, a quarter moon, a magical hand. This composition may depict the explosion of a giant star in the year 1054, an event that has also been chronicled in the history books of that time in Europe, China and Japan. Height: about 24 inches, Chaco Culture National Historical Park (New Mexico), Anasazi Culture.

Right: The Spiral, a universal motif and symbol of fertility. It also occurs in European, Siberian and South American petroglyphs, in the Sahara and Australia, from the Magdalenian Age to the Middle Ages. This is a detail of a basket, Basketmaker II, MVM.

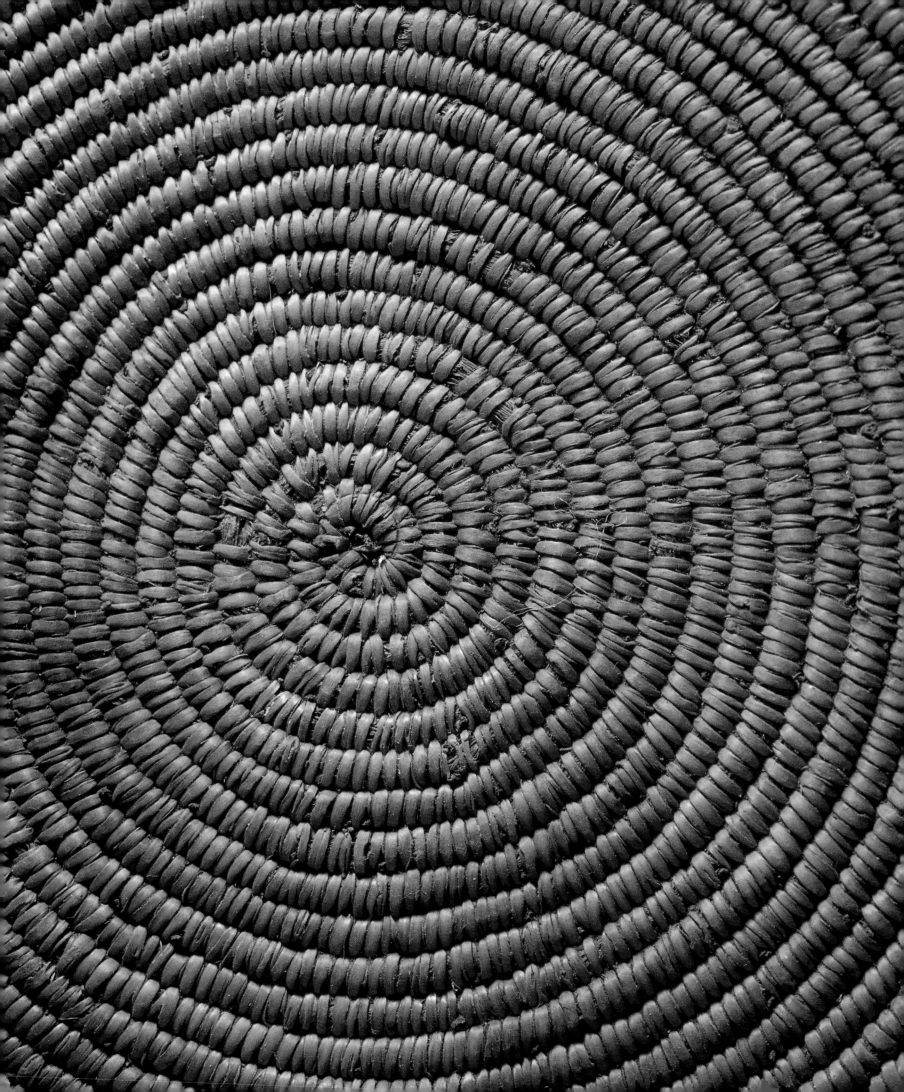

who comprise humankind: One view emphasizes the differences between peoples, the other concentrates on common features; one looks at diversity, the other at communality and a shared heritage. It is necessary to defend the latter approach in order to try to fit Southwest Indian cultures into the developmental history of our world, thereby illustrating that these other cultures are, after all, part of us too.

The historian Elie Faure has put into words the attitude with which we should approach ancient cultures:

> Whether or not one perceives it, whether or not one welcomes it, there is a universal communality which united all of man's acts and ideas not only in space but primarily in time. This intuitive, always present perception of time is after all the greatest gift available to us with which to grasp the inner meaning of all that the passage of the world has left behind, like a river leaves its alluvium. One can understand everything if one returns to the source. An African carving and a Greek marble sculpture are not as far apart as one may think.

> (*L'Espirit des Formes*, 1939)

The "True" Americans

Over a period of more than 10 millennia, Asian peoples crossed the land bridge from Siberia to Alaska, gradually moving south. The first inhabitants of the North American Southwest were Indian people whose cultures had their origins in prehistory, in the dark source from which many peoples sprang. About 2,000 years ago they began to settle in permanent communities and became the first hunters and farmers, potters and architects, craftsmen and artists. They created petroglyphs, utilizing a considerable range of images, multilayered, often mysterious and not understood even today. Universally symbolic shapes permeate these pictographs. The people were given such names as Clovis or Folsom, Basketmakers, Hohokam, Mogollon, Anasazi, City Builders, or (in Spanish) *Pueblos*.

The edges of the Colorado Plateau are still inhabited by those Pueblo Indians who call themselves the Zuni and the Hopi, said to be descendants of those Pueblo Indians who vanished in the 14th century. Similarly it is said that the Pima and Papago Indians of central and southwestern Arizona are descended from the Hohokam. As yet, however, there is no proof that this is so.

Be that as it may, it is certain that each of these peoples has preserved customs and rituals that predate the arrival of the Spaniards in the 16th century, in that time American archaeologists refer to as "prehistoric." In this way modern Pueblos are also able to tell us something about the past, a past that is seductive in its rich material culture and its wealth of ideas.

Left: Spirals made of yucca fibers, spirals in rock—two materials, a single world view: the endless circuitous movement of a star, the universe, of life. Spiral etched into sandstone. Diameter: about 10 inches. Signal Hill, Mountain Section of Saguaro National Monument (Arizona).

This book should not be approached as a strictly scientific work. It is primarily a book about art, recognizing universality in design, and the common foundation of all great cultures that have blossomed all over the world from the beginning of time to the present. In fact today a Mimbres pot, with its dynamic design, its captivating stylization, seems remarkably contemporary, and its artistry reveals the same purpose underlying all human creativity: the integration of man into the natural world in which he lives.

Many studies have been published dealing with American Southwest cultures in general, or focusing on one culture or another. The opinions and points of view conveyed, however, are often contradictory, and it has become difficult to establish consistent chronologies and to weigh the many hypotheses, theories and facts against one another. Linda S. Cordell, in one of the best syntheses available on the subject, noted in 1984: "The professional literature of southwestern archaeology of the 1980s reflects a healthy diversity of opinion in interpretation, and heated arguments about the nature of past cultures abound."

Since the 1950s the number of archaeological excavations have multiplied. Americans are increasingly conscious of their native past and are intensifying the search for the original inhabitants of their country. On the one hand, they recognize the necessity of providing a young country, a country of immigrants and emigres, with a distant past. On the other hand, they are beginning to understand the spiritual importance of the heritage left them by the Indian people. These native people were rightly called "the first Americans" by C.W. Ceram, whose study has become a classic since its first publication. Indians, especially the Indians of the Southwest, provide America with a prehistory and a history, a past, roots and a foundation.

Where once white pioneers engaged in violent conflict with the Indian people, and nearly killed them off by introducing contagious diseases and removing them from their homelands, Americans are now making an effort to treat Indian people justly. They study Indian cultures and lifestyles, have created large museum collections of cultural artifacts and have founded centers for comparative studies. Mesa Verde Park, site of the most impressive monuments of prehistoric Pueblo culture in Colorado, was established in 1906 and attracts an impressive number of tourists annually. Numerous museums in Arizona and New Mexico contain extensive collections of items of everyday use as well as religious pieces. Large museums with significant collections are also found in Los Angeles, New York and Washington, D.C. The number of visitors to these museums is growing as Americans become increasingly aware of the relationship between the several Indian cultures of the Southwest and other cultures worldwide. In this way the people of the United States are discovering a genuine antiquity in their history. The first American hunters and the first American farmers of the Neolithic period are in many respects similar to prehistoric and early historic peoples in other parts of the world.

Left: Spider Rock at the rear of Canyon de Chelly (Arizona). The 1000-foot-high sandstone column had symbolic meaning to the Indian People. In the universe every shape reveals the power of the gods; its unique beauty is additional proof of their invisible presence.

Above: Owl, basalt sculpture; a utilitarian object (toy) and also cult figure. Height: 3.72 inches. Found south of Tucson (Arizona), Hohokam Culture, AFM.

Parallels

In this volume, the primary goal is to illustrate the richness of the ancient Indian cultures of the Southwest, of which too little is known even today. These examples of pottery, baskets and petroglyphs will provide the reader with numerous parallels to what is generally known about, for instance, prehistoric European cultures. Corresponding motifs and symbols, used individually or as parts of subtle compositions, exist in large numbers: spirals, ladders, labyrinths, magical handprints, suns, undulating snake lines and others. Although created by very different peoples, their visual remains are remarkably similar.

Apart from architecture and rock paintings, the most extraordinary works of art are the pottery made by the Mogollon, Hohokam and Pueblo Indians. Their beautiful stylized motifs, maintained through 14 centuries, elevate them beyond pure art to become part of life itself. The Indian people do not actually see them as artistic creations, but as a means of placating the spirits, linking them with life in its many manifestations, uniting them with a specific environment, the fantastic high desert plateau region of the Southwest. Their creations seem totally modern; the shallow bowl decorated with a stylized lizard or the copper bell used in rituals, for instance, represent a transformation of reality, not the mere representation of a familiar object. Whether painted, etched or sculpted, there is a surprising degree of "agreement" between the symbols of Southwest Indian people and the rich, plastic vocabulary of human life elsewhere.

Beyond a doubt, the tribes of the Southwest had full access to the sophisticated cultures to the south, particularly those of Meso-America. For this reason, many scholars prefer to view them as subcultures, derived from or influenced by the high cultures of ancient Mexico. The Southwest tribes have, however, unique local characteristics directly connected to their extraordinary natural environment, the Four Corners area in Utah, Colorado, Arizona and New Mexico—with its endless variety of natural wonders. It is all the more surprising, therefore, that it was the Pueblos who developed a universal, archetypal spiritual life.

That which permeates and motivates humanity is, in the last analysis, the search for the eternal, life beyond death, which is also the search for our origins, the lost paradise of the Garden of Eden. In his mythology, the Pueblo Indian is born in the center of the earth. He works his way up to the light in stages to worship the life-giving sun, whose bright light washes over the dark shadow. His *kivas*, the ceremonial houses, are round, half subterranean—representative of mother earth and symbol of the sun. The Pueblo cliff dwellings, suspended between heaven and earth, halfway between the earth's core and the face of the sun, between light and dark, are transitional spaces between yesterday and tomorrow.

The Pueblo is aware of his vulnerability within the universe. He is conscious that his moment is brief and that his future is inexorably linked with manifold, unforeseen and

Left: A female figure chipped into the rock, denoted by the triangle. Height: 28.8 inches, Tsankawi, Bandelier National Monument (New Mexico).

Right: Lower jaws of deer with painted-on lines, X's and suns in the colors red, black, green and yellow, which symbolize the four cardinal directions, thus hunt and religious motifs are combined. Length: 4.8–7.8 inches. Hohokam Culture, ASM.

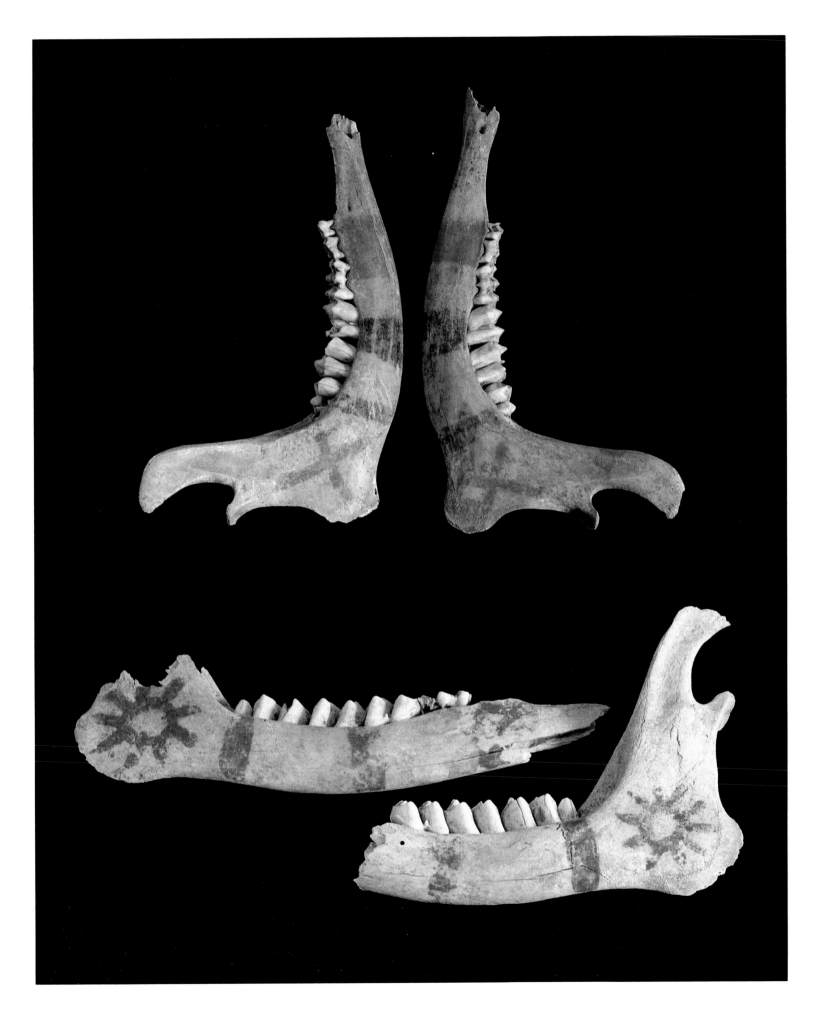

unforeseeable natural events. He is an integral part of nature because he knows that all organic and inorganic elements of his environment stand in the service of the spirits that control the world.

In his fashion, the Pueblo Indian knows that he is at the mercy of the whims of the gods. As thoughtfully as the Greeks, the Pueblos searched in their daily lives and through their rituals for the proper balance between too much and too little, revealing a natural generosity toward their environment and respect for the order of the cosmos. The gods/spirits created an ideal, perfect, unassailable geometry to which humans had to submit or accept the consequences. This geometry reaches its highest level of perfection in the structure of Pueblo Bonito in Chaco Canyon (New Mexico), a semicircle with more than 30 round *kivas*, the most remarkable relic in the Southwest.

The Indian tribes of the Southwest were peace-loving; all of their artifacts, tools made of stone or other materials, items for everyday use or religious purposes, are indicative of this. The "warriors" depicted on black or dark brown stone, armed with lances and bows, with their broad, often richly decorated shields, are undoubtably part of religious, cultic scenes celebrating the father sun, the return of hunters laden with game or the planting and harvesting of the fields. Through their reverence for their sources of sustenance, the animals and plants that sustained them or that they used for medicinal purposes, these Indian people showed us their belief in community, within or outside of their own clan. Religious, peaceable, the Pueblo Indians used their art as a medium to illustrate that the "other" is always just another side of ourselves.

On the scorched cliffs of the Southwest, the human form is never seen in isolation; man is confronted by the sun or perhaps by an animal. Unlike the rock carvings and paintings of the Magdalena or the Sahara, the figures etched in or painted on the rocks here are never alone.

Left: Pictograph of a human figure. A familiar and at the same time mysterious figure with a feather headdress, hands raised in an expression of peace and agreement. It is reminiscent of similar figures found among the petroglyphs of other cultures in Val Camonica (Italy), Siberia, the Sahara and Australia. Height: 8.8 inches. Chaco Canyon (New Mexico).

Right: The sun on the limb of a saguaro. These giant cacti can grow to a height of 50 feet. In similar form the radiating sun symbol can be found stylized on pottery or chipped into stone. Saguaro National Monument, Tucson (Arizona).

Pages 26-27: View of the Green River as it flows through Canyonlands National Park (Utah), created in 1964. The river was given its name in the 16th century by the Spaniards, impressed by the bordering vegetation, rare in the parched landscape, which was reflected in the water.

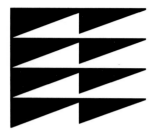# THE EXTERIOR WORLD

On the North American continent the Southwest is the land of natural wonders, a succession of unique and beautiful landscapes, full of geographic contrasts in form and color. Photographs of these enchanting vistas have been endlessly reproduced. Yet despite this familiarity, in the presence of this grandeur the emotions and sensations are never dulled.

This in large part explains the special bond *Homo americanus* has with nature, conquering a horizon that is always without boundaries, a space that is constantly expanding. Nature's changeable aspect is visible here, mythological, if not mythic: the terraces of the sulfur springs of Yellowstone; 3,000-year-old trees at Yosemite and Sequoia, reaching 160 to 200 feet into the sky; the chasm of the 5,280-foot-deep Grand Canyon; the rose, mauve, violet and deep red sandstone peaks and towers of Bryce Canyon; the red rock arches and natural bridges of Utah; the silent, towering cliffs—seat of the spirits—of Monument Valley in Navajo country; the white gypsum dunes, the largest gypsum desert in the world, glittering in the sun at White Sands (New Mexico).

An encounter with this overwhelming environment is less likely to be an intimate experience than a confrontation with something beyond human scale. The modern American who came from Europe and was formed by his North American environment, unconsciously shaped by the nature of the land, found his way back to the religious and mystical position of these sedentary Indians of the past whose lives were rooted in the nature of things.

This impact of the landscape is especially and immediately obvious in the Southwest, particularly in the four states that more or less cover the geographic territory in which the ancient Indian cultures developed: Utah, Colorado, New Mexico and Arizona. The extraordinary is common here. The earth turns under the starry sky of a glittering, clear night and the bright daily rotation of the sun, against which objects seem to move along a red, glowing horizon. The spirit of time and space is mysteriously present in the fragrant, sensual rustling of the brush, the unreal, charming shapes, the play of the wind in the sword-shaped leaves of the yucca, the cliffs that glow and crumble away, the unexpected, glorious colors of desert plants after a thunderstorm. Country such as this draws people into its spell. The nomad established his circle here, his hunting grounds; the sedentary man his foundations. This territory, arid and glowing with heat, is also fruitful; like every other desert it is remarkably fertile.

Right: Bryce Canyon (Utah), at an elevation of about 2,800 feet, presents one of the most beautiful natural landscapes in the world. The remarkable coloration of the rock is due to its composition of iron (red and brown) and manganese (violet).

Ideal Site

It is hardly surprising then that the "first American" came into being in this open country, established his societies here and, in a development parallel to the growth of the great religions of Central and South America, erected the structures of his thinking and his faith. Although he borrowed aspects of these southern cultures, he adapted and reshaped them, enriching them with his own contributions and refining them through the centuries. In this way he transformed the remarkable, fascinating landscape into an inhabited country. Since the creation, the spirits that formed the world have lived in these places—violet, gold, red, white, eroded and eroding, *alive*—they are the preferred sites of natural powers, able to take on these shapes and colors in order to exercise their power, their harsh and beautiful harmony.

The horizontal and vertical dimensions clash, the proportions are vast, beyond comprehension; one visual shock follows so closely upon the next that their combined effect is dulled until the unusual becomes familiar. The grandiose grips us in this place, we are drawn to it. The development of the Pueblo people is analogous to the development of the landscape: The individual developed and in the process he mastered his environment. A delicate symbiosis exists between a land that is beyond comprehension and the human soul, an isolated being. The various Indian cultures of the Southwest illustrate the way a people develop: On the first level man is shaped by the reality of regional geography; on the second level he subjugates the land so that the group may thrive. A similar, classic example is Egypt, whose remarkable civilization is intimately connected with the Nile.

Today the Navajo, who migrated to the Southwest in the 15th and 16th centuries, as well as those people recognized by scholars as the descendants of the Anasazi, the Zuni and the Hopi, continue to be shaped by the land, despite the modern era they now live in. Rituals and traditions that have survived for centuries not only give shape to their daily lives but also characterize the way they perceive reality.

The Southwest

Geographically the southwestern United States encompasses that area between the peaks of the Rocky Mountains and the Pacific Ocean. Culturally, however, it is generally restricted to an area that includes all or part of only four states: Arizona, New Mexico, southwestern Colorado and southern Utah. By chance, this modern perception of the boundaries underscores the uniformity of the area which exists despite its astonishing geographic diversity.

Although the boundaries within which the ancient Indian cultures developed are vague, they circumscribe about 650 square miles. The designated area is larger than most of Europe

Left: Mimbres pot, black on white, with a stylized lizard. The circular lines call to mind the shimmering heat in which this animal lives. Diameter: about 4 inches. Mimbres Valley (New Mexico), Mogollon Culture (E.H. Morris Collection), UCM.

Above: Horned toad (*Phrynosoma platyrhinos*), a reptile common to the arid Southwest.

combined. The Colorado Plateau extends along the northern extreme of the square. It is the famous "wonderland of America," containing six national parks—Grand Canyon, Zion, Bryce Canyon, Canyonland, Arches and Petrified Forest—the land of natural wonders, also called Canyon Country, Canyonland or the Four Corners Area. At a median elevation of 5,280 feet it is traversed by a complex system of canyons that cut across flat plateaus, called "mesas" (tables) by the Spaniards who explored the area in the 16th century. The geological process that has formed the land has been ongoing for the last 10 millennia.

The Colorado Plateau consists mainly of sandstone, limestone and shale. Occasionally, especially in the south, cooled lava streams can be found, covered with numerous cinder cones. Springs are plentiful, fed by groundwater collected on a bed of impervious shale and filtered through sandstone deposits. The vastness and barrenness of this land is so extraordinary that Mesa Verde, which, with its 800 ruins is second only to Chaco Canyon in the number of its dwellings, was not discovered until 1888 and then purely by accident by two cowboys looking for stray cattle.

The mountainous interior of the land, a consequence of volcanic activity and erosion, is forested at the higher elevations. This area of trees is generally in the shape of a *Y*, whose arms point slightly west and east, that forms a natural boundary between New Mexico and the great central plains—an area where many different Indian cultures developed. The mountains rise to a height of 13,200 feet (the highest peak in Arizona is Humphreys Peak, 12,744 feet; in New Mexico the highest mountain is Wheeler Peak, 13,236 feet). As indicated by the location of ruins, the riverine areas among the mountains were most heavily populated. Current scholarship considers these areas the original territory of the Pueblo Indians.

In the south, arid and semi-arid land, the Sonora and Chihuahua deserts, stretches to the northern Mexican border. It is in these desert stretches that the first contacts with Meso-Americans were made. Naturally occurring north-south corridors, interspersed with more verdant areas, made trade and cultural exchange possible, as evidenced by the architectural styles and ornamentation found on pottery in the region. In Mexico, Casas Grandes, located approximately 90 miles south of the New Mexico border, was a flourishing communication center from the 11th to the 14th century, providing for exchanges between the civilization flourishing in Central America and the Pueblo cultures. Several experts have opined that, without this connection, Pueblo culture would never have achieved its high cultural *niveau*.

The ancient Indian cultures therefore developed in a land rhythmically accentuated by changeable and contrasting contours and considerable variation in altitude, more often semi-arid than desert, interspersed with many niches and oases where plant and animal life flourished. These were the places where the tribes established their communities, from which their culture expanded. In this connection, Frank Waters wrote in *Masked Gods* (1950): "Physically and metaphysically the Four Corners is indeed the heartland of America.

Above: Petroglyph representing a stylized desert mammal with a disproportionately large, round and crosshatched body, the sign of the labyrinth (progress through life) enclosed in a circle. The whole image suggests the willingness of the animal to acclimate to a difficult environment. Height: about 28 inches. Dry Fork Canyon (Utah).

Squared astronomically to space and time by the sacred peaks of the directions, it is still rigidly defined by legend and nature alike...Paradoxically it is the oldest habitation of known life in America—both animal and human, and the least populated today."

Climate

Rather than one climate, the southwest is characterized by a complex of microclimates. Flora and fauna must adapt to the constantly changing conditions that may occur within a comparatively small area. For example, while more than 16 feet of snow may fall on the north rim of the Grand Canyon, the south rim, 11 miles away, will receive only half of that amount, and the bottom of the canyon will experience no snowfall at all! Seasonal contrasts are equally drastic. The Sonora Desert in southern Arizona is, for example, one of the hottest places on earth during the summer, but its climate from November through April is very pleasant. And from April until May or June there are few deserts that can rival the Sonora for its splendid color—literally hundreds of varieties of cactus are in bloom. Rainfall in the Southwest is usually less than 20 inches annually; in desert areas the rainfall is less than 8 inches. Extremely heavy thunderstorms, however, may occur. During the summer temperatures may reach as high as 104 degrees Fahrenheit, while the winters on the Colorado Plateau can be biting cold. Spring is a time of high winds. In general, the air is unusually clear: On most days the residents of Albuquerque can see the peak of Mount Taylor, 60 miles away. By and large, the entire Southwest has a dry climate, which makes extremes of both heat and cold more bearable.

Water

Water sources played an essential role in the development of ancient Indian cultures and the availability of water determined the location of Pueblo villages. Rainfall in the Southwest is a rarity and many streams run dry. Doubtless there were more rivers at one time. John C. McGregor, in his excellent synthesis *Southwestern Archaeology* (2nd ed., 1965), describes the most important of them. Many have dried up over the centuries, or, like the Gila River in New Mexico and Arizona, may run only part of the year. The many villages with ruins of extensive irrigation systems are proof that there was once a wealth of water.

Two large rivers still flow, majestic and mighty, important arteries both in the past and the present that have played an important role in the religious and secular lives of the Pueblo people. The first is the Colorado River, with its source in the Rocky Mountains, which flows into the Gulf of California. The Green River is one of its tributaries, while the San Juan, Little Colorado and Gila rivers flow steadily into it. The other major river is the Rio Grande del Norte. It also has its source in Colorado, in the San Juan Mountains, and with its major

Above: Detail of a Mimbres pot, black on white. A stylized bird, part of its body denoted with a labyrinth motif, symbolizes the infinity of the sky. Diameter: 15.36 inches. Mimbres Valley (New Mexico), MMA.

Pages 34-35: The environment of the past and present. The fauna include reptiles, colorful birds, sparring mule deer in Capitol Reef National Park (Utah). Flora—yucca and cactus flowers—here in May and June, transform the desert into a sea of glowing colors. Petroglyphs, of a reptile surrounded by mysterious signs, hand and foot prints, from Newspaper Rock, Petrified Forest National Park (Arizona) and Snake (Utah). On the Mimbres pot two fish fight over a worm. Diameter: 12.08 inches, UCM.

tributary, the Pecos River, flows south through New Mexico and then along the Texas border, emptying finally into the Gulf of Mexico.

The Colorado and its tributaries have cut deeply into the plateau for millennia, giving the area its unmistakable physiography, the continuous, deeply cut canyons. The Rio Grande, on the other hand, flows through a valley that is wide in places and covered with rich alluvial mud. Many settlements are found here, both ancient and modern. In southern Arizona the Gila River and its tributary, the Salt River, create a similar geography in what was the homeland of the ancient Hohokam people.

Other areas are far less hospitable than these fertile regions. Walnut Canyon near Flagstaff, Arizona, for instance, with its approximately 350 cliff dwellings, is today a semi-arid desert and the canyon is totally dry, but in the 11th century it was covered by fertile soil and supported a variety of native plants that in turn sustained abundant animal life.

The Colorado River was once wild and knew no boundaries. Today its floods are controlled by enormous dams and reservoirs. Until the 20th century, it was one of the mightiest rivers on the American continent, carrying with it as much soil and rock as water, which accounts for its Spanish name, Colorado, meaning "red." It was described by the early explorers as "too thick to drink and too thin to plow." The river's daily freight consisted of about 500,000 tons of sand, mud, fragmented sandstone, clay, lime and granite, and its volume exceeded 100,000 cubic meters (130,000 cubic yards) per second. The water from the Colorado River is hard and has an unpleasant taste. Indians did not drink it. They drew from the springs at the edge of the canyons for drinking water, and this is where they located their fields. The wildly turbulent waters of the Colorado, which flowed with a tremendous velocity and at a depth of about 4300 feet, represented the power of the life principle to Indian people.

Flora

The flora of the southwest is to a large extent a function of elevation. The distribution of plants falls within two major climatic zones:

1. Sonora Zone: 0–6,600 feet

   a. Lower Sonora Zone
   Desert shrubs and desert grasslands (cacti, creosote, mesquite and yucca)
   b. Upper Sonora Zone
   Pinyon-Juniper plant group (bear grass, agave)

Right: Fossilized wood in Petrified Forest National Park (Arizona), a desert landscape in colors that stimulate the spirit. Confronted with such landscapes, where reality may seem inseparable from the supernatural, one understands why the Indian, in order to live in harmony with himself and the surrounding natural world, decorated his artifacts with highly stylized shapes as an expression of the invisible and dynamic world order.

2. Montane Zone: above 6,600 feet a. Lower Montane Zone
Pinyon-Juniper plant group (juniper, scrub oak, pinyon pine)
b. Upper Montane Zone
Spruce-Douglas Fir (ponderosa pine, douglas fir, oaks)

The plants are remarkable for their ability to survive in adverse conditions. They are able to protect themselves from the sun and from dehydration; leaves and thorns serve to store moisture. After even a light rain they bloom in colorful profusion and reproduce. Among these plants are 140 varieties of cactus, the most amazing of the southwestern plants in both appearance and structure. Among them are the organpipe cactus (*Lemaireocereus thurberi*) and the saguaro, candelabra cactus (*Carnegiea pipantea*), the largest cactus in the world. The latter can reach a height of nearly 50 feet and many weigh as much as seven tons, with a lifespan of 150–200 years. Within its bulk this cactus can store thousands of quarts of water and in this way can survive one or even two years without a drop of rain.

For the Pueblo people, the cactus is a symbol of life and death, beneficial and threatening. The cactus must be respected even when it is used for food or medicinal purposes. It is never depicted on pottery or petroglyphs, not even in stylized form.

Then and Now

The level of moisture throughout the region varies: Those slopes facing north and east generally have more water than those facing south or west. For this reason we find the Pueblo ruins on the northern and eastern slopes. The two walls of a canyon often contrast sharply: One will be barren, the other fertile.

It must be remembered that the physical appearance of some regions has changed drastically through the centuries. The yellow pine forests that once surrounded Chaco Canyon, for example, site of the most impressive Pueblo ruins, have completely disap-

Above left: Miniature clay figurine of a bird. Height: 1.12 inches. Anasazi Culture, MNA. Center: Ceramic container in the shape of a deer, black on white, in the Tularosa style, with double openings; the liqid was poured out of the mouth. Length: 4.8 inches. CCP. Right: Clay figurine representing a four-footed animal. Length: 2.12 inches. Sinagua Culture, MNA.

peared and have been replaced by junipers and stunted firs. Soil conditions have deteriorated due to a variety of factors, among them over-cultivation and the destruction of the timber stands for firewood and building material. Prolonged irrigation of the poorly drained soil caused concentrations of salt and other minerals to develop. The sedentary people who built these communities were consequently forced to relocate their fields and villages frequently. The large number of Pueblo ruins in the Four Corners area of the southwestern states can certainly be explained in this way, rather than by massive increases in population.

Finally, it should be noted that due to natural conditions—drought and aridity—fragile archaeological material such as wood, bones, seeds, animal remains etc. have been well preserved to the present day. In terms of quantity of artifacts found, the Southwest exceeds all other parts of the United States.

The large number of bones of various species of animals found in Mesa Verde National Park shows us that animal life has changed little over the years. The animals most heavily represented in the forests and valleys of the Southwest are deer, pronghorn antelope, mountain sheep, coyote and fox; mountain lions and wolves are now rare, however. There are also numerous rodents, such as hare, rabbits and squirrels, and reptiles, such as snakes and lizards. The presence of many birds is attested to by innumerable bones of, for example, golden eagles, doves and quail, and excavations have turned up a rich palette of feathers, which were used for religious ceremonies. It is also known that the Pueblos domesticated turkeys, also apparently for religious purposes.

Thus, paradoxically, the Southwest, consisting largely of semi-arid desert, produces an abundance of plants and animals, which, prior to the 16th century, was probably even more plentiful. It is an extraordinary, thriving landscape, a prerequisite for cultural growth.

Above: Pictograph of a turkey, domesticated by the Anasazi for its feathers (used in religious ceremonies), irregularly incised, chipped and picked. Height: 18.4 inches. Found near the Visitor Center of Chaco Canyon National Historical Park (New Mexico).

Pages 40-41: Thunderstorm over the Grand Canyon (Arizona). View from Mather Point in the National Park at 7,000 feet. Lightning, as the harbinger of rain, was stylized as a zig-zag line on southwestern pottery and in petroglyphs.

INNER WORLDS

The American Southwest displays a multitude of physical contrasts, which the Pueblo people internalized. In a universe of fire and color, of immense rock formations shimmering along the deceptively shifting horizon, the human spirit must either intervene to bring order or perish. The quality of the tools and utensils made by the Pueblos reflects this desire for order. The Mimbres clay pots are among the most innovative creations found on the American continent, both in terms of artistic merit and symbolic importance. The emphasis is on stylized composition that utilizes the curved interior and exterior surfaces of the vessel and creates worlds that are complete in themselves. There is, however, an opening to the outside, created by means of skillfully worked vanishing points that meet beyond the represented motif.

In this country the high and low, broad and narrow, smooth and jagged, supernatural and mortal meet in a cosmology contained in symbols and images. In the cosmology of the Pueblo people, the Southwest represents a synthesis of the world, the summation of the six primary divisions so beloved, for example, by the Chinese: four horizontal and two vertical directions, with contrasting upper and lower levels.

Colors

In this red-, violet-, gold- and ochre-colored world the Native American, from early on, felt the need to reduce his environment to geometry. The Romanian religious scholar Mircea Eliade noted in this regard:

> Space is divisible according to its position relative to the human body; it all depends on whether it extends before or behind, to the right or the left, above below him. The various possibilities of an *orientatio* grow from a primordial experience, namely the feeling of having been 'thrown' into an apparently boundless, unknown and threatening space, for one cannot exist long with the vertigo that comes of disorientation. The experience of space as being organized around a 'center' gives broader significance to the division and partitioning of territories, communities and dwellings and their cosmological symbolism.
>
> (*A History of Religious Ideas,* 1976)

To the Pueblo people these divisions were indicated by special colors. This was also the case with the Aztecs and the Maya. Although the significance of the colors varies from tribe

Right: Small clay figure with legs drawn up and hands folded over the chest; at left actual size (2.72 inches high), right enlarged, with traces of yellow, red and turquoise colors (limonite, hematite and malachite). Of indefinite style, the nose was pinched out of the clay while the eyes and mouth are indicated by simple slits. This piece of art is both clumsy in its simplified form and intriguingly mysterious. It was found in a grave and probably depicts a corpse. Region of the Little Colorado River (Arizona), Anasazi Culture, ASM.

to tribe, the colors always establish a relationship with the environment. The Hopi and Zuni, for example, designate each of the six divisions with its own sacred color: Yellow represents the north, blue the west, red the south and white the east. Black signifies the center of the earth below and many colors in combination indicate the zenith above.

Colors have played an important role in all cultures, in everyday life as well as in religious and ceremonial practices. Presumably this same scheme was already used by prehistoric peoples; we know this was so in the case of Meso-American cultures. (Similarly, the Buddhist mandelas are divided into four equal sections, each representing one of the points of the compass. Each of these divisions is assigned a color: blue, green, red and yellow.) The symbolism of color characterizes not only the geographic environment, but all levels of being and knowledge, cosmological, psychological, mystic. Innumerable treatises have dealt with this theme from antiquity to the present. It is surprising to think that 20th-century artists have, through experimentation with color and color theories, merely found their way back to the symbolism of the Pueblo Indians and other cultures.

In the Southwest, nature is above all a feast of color. The skies are crystal blue, violet, lead gray, pink, a glowing dark red. The ground and the rock is pink, aubergine, ochre-colored, satiny, golden. Color in this context is virtually an abstraction. Its boldness doesn't signify otherworldliness, but precisely the opposite, namely the present, the terrible reality of dust and heat under a shimmering sky, a red, glowing horizon. The southwestern landscape seems more true, more believable, when viewed from a distance, inexhaustible and unfolding in all of its splendor, continually recreated in more perfect form.

There may be other places on earth with similarly complex physical features, but few other places can exhibit such an astonishingly rich palette of colors and forms as the American Southwest, a vision so full of life and simultaneously so barren. Only art can express such a reality.

It is known today that colors by themselves do not signify anything. In great art, color is dependent on the form that gives it shape. Together they make a whole—content and container. When the surroundings are lost in unreality and appear strange, barely familiar, the form is eclipsed by the color. In that case, the color more clearly defines the form, and the form lends to the color a heightened intensity. It is not accidental that Spanish terms for forms—such as mesa, butte, canyon and arroyo—evolved in the Southwest into words describing land formations.

Such a country is perfectly made to receive the mystical fire of man, to nourish legends, which join men in a universal cosmography. It is beyond doubt that from the time men first appeared in the Southwest the landscape played a vital role in the creation of myths and legends. Geographic features, past and present, are explained through the activities of supernatural heroes, giants, gods and mythical animals. In the eyes of the Pueblo Indians

Left: Petroglyphs with a stylized deer, positive impression of a magic hand and a human figure within a circle, which undoubtedly symbolizes the sun and the entire universe. A language of shapes extends across the rocks, mingling daily routine and religious life. Diameter of the circle: about 28 in. Betatakin, Navajo National Monument (Arizona).

Page 46: Delicate Arch, one of the most beautiful natural arches in the world, is about 28 feet high and 22 feet wide, in Arches National Park (Utah), which contains more than 90 of these sandstone formations. This "artwork" is created by the natural process of erosion by water, wind, sun and frost. Right: a fossilized piece of wood in Petrified Forest National Park (Arizona), where hundreds of petrified tree trunks, visible above soil level, can be seen. Iron, manganese, carbon and other minerals have imparted these unusual colors to the silica that was deposited in the wood as it lay buried under mud and water.

the color and shape of the land signify fate, the sometimes silent, sometimes rumbling voice of the godhead, the totality of the spirits of the earth and heaven.

Alfonso Ortiz writes in his introduction to Vol. 9, *Southwest* (Handbook of North American Indians):

> The land is so hot in the summer that the air just above it quivers before the naked eye, as if there were ghostly presences about in broad daylight. At the hottest time of day the vibrations of the earth can cause objects in the distance, or even the horizon itself, to waver so much that one cannot trust one's own eyes. Sometimes the pressures of air, heat, and sand unite in an explosive combination that may send as many as six whirlwinds at a time dancing across the landscape.

The Hohokam peoples contemplated these whirlwinds and recorded their impressions on petroglyphs and pottery.

The Presence of the Gods

In the '20s Swiss psychiatrist Carl Jung visited the contemporary Pueblo Indians at Taos, New Mexico. He tells the following story:

> As I sat on the roof with Ochwia Biano and the sun rose higher and higher in the sky, the rays blinding, he said, pointing to the sun: "Is not he who goes there our father? How can it be otherwise? How can another be God? Nothing can exist without the sun." His already evident agitation increased even more and, searching for words, he finally called out: "What does a man want alone in the mountains? He cannot even make a fire without Him." I asked him if he did not think the sun was a flaming sphere formed by an invisible God. My question did not seem to surprise him, much less to irritate him. It apparently called forth no reaction whatever in him, and he did not even find my question foolish. It left him completely cold. I had the feeling that I had come up against an unscalable wall. The only answer I received was: "The sun is God. Everyone can see that."
>
> (*Memories, Dreams, Reflections*, 1971)

In the Southwest nature leads man directly to the basic questions of human existence, the creation, origins. Each rock, every terrestrial phenomenon has, at present, a mythological explanation. This must have been true in the past also. The fossilized trees of Petrified Forest National Park (Arizona) are, to the Navajo, the mighty limbs of the giant Yietso who was killed by the war god. To the Paiutes of Southern Utah they are the arrows of Shinuav, the thunder god. Famous Rainbow Bridge, the largest natural bridge in the world, 330 feet high and equally as wide, represents petrified lovers to the Rainbow People; the Navajo see in it the god who brings rain.

Page 47: Early spring along the Colorado River near the town of Moab (Utah). Ice floats on the river, last witness to a cold winter.

George Dumezil wrote:

A country without legends is condemned to freeze to death, but a people without myths is already dead. In fact, the purpose of this special kind of story-telling that myths represent is to give dramatic expression to the ideology according to which a society lives, the recognized values and ideals which generation after generation strives to keep alive in the consciousthought of its people—first, their being and organization, as well as the elements, relationships, harmonies and tensions which go into this, and, finally, to establish the transmitted rules and practices which hold the whole structure together."

(*Heur et malheur du guerrier*, 1985)

The ancient Indian cultures of the Southwest left behind no written testimonies; there are neither texts nor codes. We can draw certain conclusions, however, by studying modern Pueblo, Zuni and Hopi people, and even the Navajo, who also have a long tradition and have many cultural elements in common with the Pueblo societies. The architecture (in particular *kivas*, the round ceremonial structures) and the art of pottery-making are proof of the constancy of form and spirit that provide access to the inner worlds of the first Americans.

The numerous creation myths of the Hopi, Zuni and other Indian tribes of the Southwest are multilayered and very original. Like the mythologies of other cultures, they too rely most heavily on the personification of animals and natural forces that embody supernatural spirits. The myths of contemporary Pueblos, especially those of the Pueblo elders, are archaic but very much alive as forms of the creative imagination of which the pottery and petroglyphs provide abundant evidence. The coherence is complete; the basic expressions so necessary for life can be traced through the centuries in the form of earth, rain, death and the symbol for lightning.

There is much still to be discovered about these legends. Although there are numerous fragmentary studies, they all too often fall somewhere between poetry and truth.

The Creation Myth

One example is the modern version of the Hopi creation myth as summarized in *Prehistoric Indians*, by F.A. Barnes and Michaeline Pendleton:

In the Beginning, there was a great nothingness, a blackness without space or time. And then there was Tawa, the Creator, whose power was the Sun. Out of the blackness, Tawa created all the stars and planets of the Universe, and He created the Earth. And so the Earth would not be alone, Tawa reached deep inside the Earth and planted insect creatures, ants and beetles, and things that crawl.

Mockingbird gave them Tawa's laws and told them of his desires. But the insect creatures didn't understand how Tawa wanted them to live. They fought and quarrelled among themselves. This displeased and sorrowed Tawa so He sent Spider Grandmother to show the insect creatures the way to a better world so that they might live as Tawa wanted.

Spider Grandmother showed the way to a new world Tawa had created closer to the surface of the Earth. As they came into this new world, some of the creatures found that their bodies had changed. Now some of them were wolves, rabbits, coyotes, bear, deer, and all the other animals that live on Earth. But they still didn't understand what Great Tawa wanted, and again they fought and killed each other. Again Tawa sent Spider Grandmother to them.

This time Spider Grandmother led all the animal creatures to a third world that lay just below the surface of the Earth. In this world, some of the animals became men and these Spider Grandmother taught how to live in peace, to plant corn, and to worship Tawa and all the lesser gods.

For a time, all was good and Tawa was pleased. But there were sorcerers among the people, evil men who tempted them away from the life Tawa wanted them to live. The people started to spend their time stealing and gambling, fighting and killing. They neglected their work and they no longer worshipped the gods. But a few of the people did not follow the evil sorcerers. They tended their crops and made their prayer sticks and lived peacefully with each other.

When Tawa saw what was happening, for a third time He sent Spider Grandmother to them. She led the people who had resisted evil up to a small opening in the world. As the people came out of this *sipapu* hole onto the surface of the Earth into the light of Tawa's Sun, Mockingbird changed them into all the different people that now live on Earth. Some were Hopi, some Zuni, some White Men—and they all went their different directions to live as Tawa decreed in the valleys and forests and mountains of the Earth.

So say the Hopi. The legend has lived in the smoke of *kiva* fires since before the memory of the oldest man. It is a tale passed down from the Ancient Ones—the Anasazi.

The natural configurations of the Southwest are the product of heaven and of the underworld. Again it is the geography that explains to a large extent the religious practices and beliefs of these ancient Indian cultures. In contrast to the many cultures that believe themselves to have originated in the heavens, the Pueblo people believe themselves to have come from the center of the world, the innermost core of the earth. After achieving various intermediate levels they reach the surface of the earth, through the *sipapu*, a small round hole in the floor of each partially subterranean *kiva*, the connection between shadow and light, earth and heaven, night and sun. When they reach the surface, cleansed and purified, a world of color and light is revealed to them. The Hopi believe the gorge of the Grand Canyon to be the widest and deepest *sipapu*, leading to a past shrouded in mist and shadow.

In the basic structure, the creation myth is part of the great universal parable. The symbolically significant concept of the *sipapu* occurs in many cultures with the same essential meaning. Mircae Eliade has said in this connection: "In Asia the universe is

Right: The white cliffs in Zion National Park (Utah). The shape of the clouds, the colors of the eroded rock, as well as the vegetation adapted to the difficult, semi-arid conditions all contribute to the immersion of the inhabitants of this country in a magical and mythological world.

perceived as a whole consisting of three layers—heaven, earth and hell—connected with one another by a central axis. This axis extends through an 'opening,' a 'hole,' through which the gods enter earth and the dead climb into the underworld. The soul of the shaman on its journeys to heaven or hell can climb up or down through this hole. The three worlds, the home of the gods, of men, and of the lord of hell, respectively, are pictured as three superimposed levels" (*A History of Religious Ideas,* 1983).

The Pueblo Indians who believed they came from inside the earth, lived, at the peak of their cultural development, in cliff dwellings suspended halfway between heaven and earth, between the floor of the canyon and its rim. Remembering that their first dwellings were pit houses, half underground like the *kivas,* their relationship with the land changed, but even where Pueblo people constructed significant structures, such as cliff dwellings, *kivas* and irrigation canals, they were not a race of architectural or engineering geniuses. They were people who relied on their experience and waged a daily battle to survive. This is the way in which these people adapted to geological and geographic reality and lived in beautiful harmony with their myths and beliefs.

The peaks of the distant, pale mauve mountains, a significant feature in a unique landscape, give the Indian people the certainty that they are the children of the life- and death-giving sun. The Southwest landscape is of such pervasive ambiguity that, although it sustains life, it becomes a deadly place if even slight errors are made in the adaptation of people struggling to survive in it. It remains an environment of minerals and living things, glorious beauty and harsh severity, horizontal and vertical dimensions that flow into one another, sharply delineated details visible in the glaring light of burning rock formations. In this place the horizon is always receding, out of reach. The 990-foot upthrust of Spider Rock in Canyon de Chelly symbolizes the emergence of the Pueblo people on their way to Taiowa, their creator.

Left: Pictograph showing a big-horned sheep pierced by three arrows. The body is divided by geometric and decorative lines, which undoubtedly have symbolic meaning. Roughly picked, the implied shapes are easily recognizable (curved horns, hooves), an effect achieved by means of finer incising. Length: 28 inches. Three Rivers Petroglyph Site, north of Alamogordo (New Mexico). There are around 5,000 petroglyphs in this historic area: animals, representations of humans, geometric and abstract shapes.

Pages 54-55: Hairpin curves of the San Juan River, one of the tributaries of the Colorado, near Mexican Hat in the southeast corner of Utah.

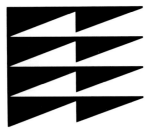 A PREHISTORY

The concept "prehistory" or "early history" is here used to encompass the history of human society from the first appearance of hominids—according to current theory about five million years ago—until the appearance of the first written texts (cuneiform characters used by the Sumarians) about 3000 B.C. or even as long ago as 8000 B.C. (based on an original text found in Central Asia in the 1960s and written in the form of geometric signs).

Human beings appeared late in the American Southwest, around 10,000 B.C. The period beginning then and extending into the Christian era is divided into two long segments: The Paleo-Indian Period and, beginning about 8000 B.C., the Archaic Period. As of approximately the birth of Christ, the Formative Period began. The term "prehistoric" is often used up through the Formative Period, which lasted into the first half of the 16th century, when Spaniards pushed into the Southwest from Mexico. They brought with them the horse, which was to become the preferred means of transportation of Indian nomads who settled in the country abandoned by the Pueblo Indians during the droughts of the 13th and 14th centuries.

Where did these first Americans, today called "Indians," come from? After decades of passionately defending contradictory theories, scholars appear to agree that the Indians' origin is Asiatic. There are certain physical characteristics that Indians share with Mongolian people: a yellow skin tone, dark eyes, straight dark hair, prominent cheek bones, and the frequent occurrence of the so-called Mongolian fold on the eyelid. Over the course of their long isolation on the American continent, however, they also developed some new characteristics, unique to American Indians, such as a narrow range of blood types, special skin pigmentation and the "shovel" shape of the incisors. Adaptation to varying geographic conditions led to further differentiation into many distinctive peoples and cultures.

Comparative paleontologic studies and artifacts found in Alaska and Siberia illustrate other significant similarities between Native Americans and prehistoric Asian people. It is now generally agreed that the people we know as Indians entered this country by crossing the Bering Straight, which is only 45 miles wide and now barely 330 feet deep. At the peak of the last ice age the water level in the oceans sank as a consequence of extensive ice formations inland, and a wide land bridge came into being as the water receded from this shallow straight. Animals had traveled this route long before human beings and had spread over both American continents, among them mammoths, mastadons, the giant sloth, bison (*Bison antiquus*), small early ancestors of horses, camels and others.

Right: View from the Colorado State Monument of the Rio Grande, which flows south through New Mexico. On the horizon are the Sandia Mountains, where between 1937 and 1941 the oldest artifacts establishing an Indian presence in the Southwest were found in Sandia Cave.

 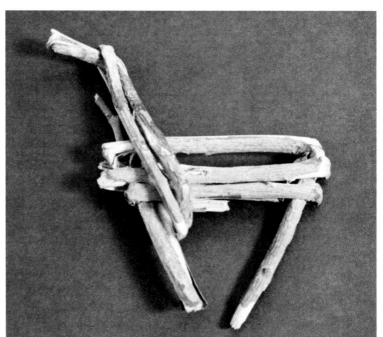

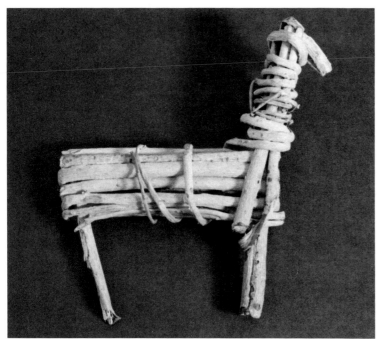 

Beyond doubt the migrations of people over the Bering Straight occurred in consecutive waves. Some of these groups reached the southernmost point of South America as early as 8000 B.C. The archaeologist C. Vance Haynes, Jr., illustrated the migrations of people in time and space utilizing sophisticated calculations (*Scientific American*, 1966), and concluded that it is probable that the population toward the end of the Paleo-Indian Period, the time of large game hunters, increased sharply and that these people traveled long distances. Within half a millennium they occupied all of North America south of the inhospitable interior ice sheet.

Geological investigations of the Bering Strait show that the sinking of the ocean level left a 330-foot wide strip of dry land during the Second Wisconsin Ice Age (about 25,000–10,000 B.C.), thereby creating, as noted, a solid land bridge between Northeast Asia and Alaska. Men and animals could populate the land strip, called "Beringia," and enter the New World "unnoticed." A further migration south, however, was not possible until the huge inland glaciers began to recede, which happened about 13,000 B.C., when an ice-free corridor opened between the western Cordilleran Glacier (approximately where the Rocky Mountains are today) and the eastern Laurentian Glacier (from the Great Lakes to the Arctic Ocean). Early theories held by American geologists dated this corridor as early as 25,000 B.C. and led to the establishment of new dating, utilizing more precise methods, which puts all sites and artifacts at no older than 12,000 years. After dating according to the AMS (accelerated mass spectometry) method, an improved carbon dating system, it was shown that California skull and bone fragments found in this area, previously thought to be perhaps 40,000 years old, are no older than 5,000 years. Even the famous caribou bone scraper, formed by human hands, that was found on the Old Crow site in Alaska, is no older than 3,500 years.

Sandia and Clovis

In the Southwest, the oldest sites with signs of human activity are Sandia and Clovis. Sandia Cave, in the Sandia Mountains near Albuquerque, New Mexico, excavated between 1937 and 1941, yielded the bones of mammoths, giant sloths, bison, horses and camels. Stone tools were found in the vicinity, especially crudely crafted flint points. The so-called Sandia point, apparently a local type, is leaf shaped and characterized by an inset at the base, which is sometimes concave, resembling the clearly fluted Clovis point, in use at the same time. These points were not arrowheads; during the Paleo-Indian period stone points were used to tip lances that were thrown with a throwing stick, or *atlatl*.

In the '30s, a site close to Clovis, New Mexico, yielded scrapers, bits of charcoal, burned bison bones, polished bone implements, knives and above all, finely worked points, from about three to five inches long, which were fluted or grooved. The intent of the groove was

Left: Several split twig figures, representing deer, each made from a single thin willow rod or from some other flexible wood. Archaic Period, 2000-1000 B.C. Clockwise from upper left: 2.6 inches high, Walnut Canyon (Arizona), MNA; 3.88 inches high, Sycamore Canyon (Arizona), ASM; 4.52 inches high, Grand Canyon National Park (Arizona), MNA; 5.8 inches, also from Grand Canyon National Park (Arizona), ASM.

undoubtedly to simplify attaching the point to the shaft of a spear. It was possible to kill the large animals of the Pleistocene Period with lances and spears: mammoths, giant sloths, bison and other animals, not all of which have become extinct. Excavations done between 1960 and 1980 at the Lehner site in southern Arizona turned up ten mammoths. Lances, spears and stone scrapers were also found there.

The Clovis or "Llano" Culture lasted from 10,000–9000 B.C. More than a hundred sites dated by means of carbon dating attest to the presence of this culture in the Southwest. Fluted points were, however, also found by the hundreds of thousands in other parts of what is now the United States, and isolated examples have been found further south. The *atlatl*, made of wood or bone, was probably also in use at this time. C.W. Ceram provides a precise description: "The atlatl is a spear thrower. The term comes to us from the Aztecs by way of the Spaniards: at'-latl. It is a short piece of hard wood, no longer than 24 inches long, with loops at one end through which the thrower gripped the atlatl, and a groove at the other end. A short spear is fitted into the groove. The atlatl itself, which in effect lengthens the throwing arm, is thrown forward in an arc. At the point of greatest velocity the spear becomes airborne with considerably more force than a spear thrown in the ordinary fashion…" (*The First American*, 1971).

The Clovis people were big-game hunters who combined technology with cunning. The places where the game was brought down and butchered were generally located at the edge of prehistoric swamps or riverbeds. Here the men lay in wait for the big mammals and then cut off their escape routes.

Folsom

The excavation of a site near Folsom, New Mexico, began in 1926. It is the best known site after Clovis and is dated from 9000 to 8000 B.C. In addition to bison bones, 1- to 3.2-inch long points known as the Folsom points were found, almost all of them fluted on both sides with skillfully worked grooves.

Like the Clovis people, the Folsom people were big-game hunters who hunted largely bison; the mammoth was extinct by this time. Ample evidence of their hunting activity is provided by the many sites where animals had been butchered, from the plains in eastern New Mexico to southern Arizona.

At the end of the Paleo-Indian Period appeared the so-called Plano Points, beginning about 8000 B.C. It is characteristic of these points that while many variations have been discovered none are fluted. Three distinct types of sites, which also yielded carefully crafted stone tools, triangular knives, scrapers and hammers, indicate a highly organized society based on the division of labor. There are permanent campsites, work areas where groups of hunters made projectile points and temporary camps used only for hunting, butchering

Above: Tool made of mammoth bone, probably used to straighten bent spear shafts. Similar objects belonging to the early Paleolithic Period have been found in Europe. Length: 10.32 inches, Murray Spring, San Pedro River Valley (Arizona), Paleo-Indian Period, Clovis Culture, 9230 B.C., ASM.

Right: Projectile points, made of flint and quartz, frequently found near mammoth and bison bones. The fourth point from the left is grooved at the base to make it easier to fasten it to the shaft. Longest point: 3.88 inches. Paleo-Indian Period, Clovis Culture, approximately 9500 B.C., ASM.

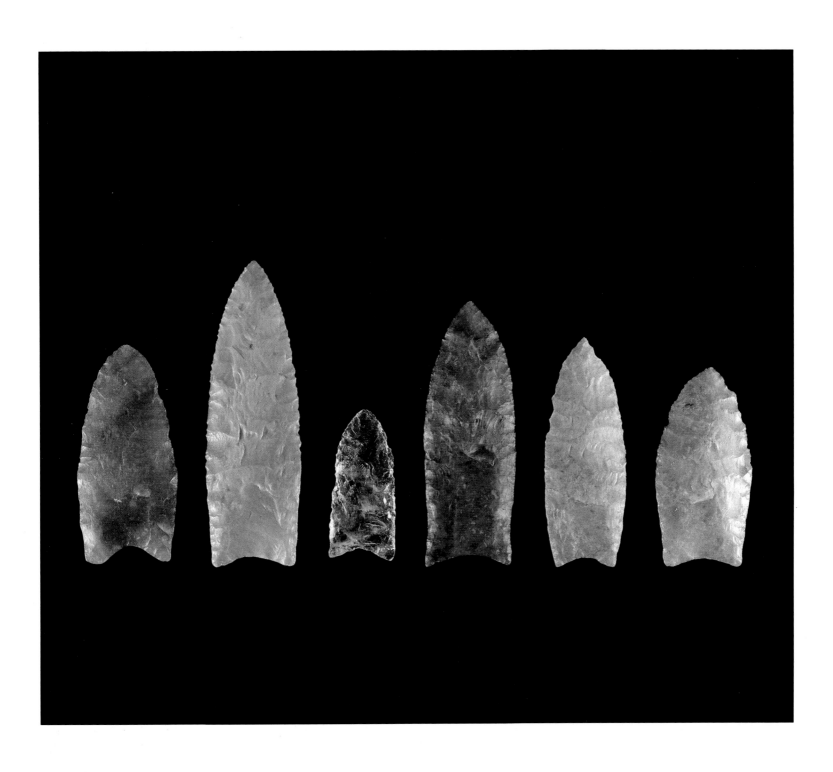

the animals, and working the skins. An "overkill" theory holds that the decimation of the giant mammals was occasioned by men. For example, the remains of a herd of bison were discovered in Plainview, Texas. They had been driven to their death over the edge of a cliff and numerous projectile points were found among their bones. It is more likely, however, that the great animals fell victim to climatic changes.

Ventana Cave

There was a significant change in the climate around 8000 B.C. connected with the receding inland glaciers. Temperatures rose and the land gradually assumed a semi-arid aspect. Plant and animal life became more sparse. A few climatically favorable microclimates remained, and here remnants of the Pleistocene (1.8 million to 10,000 years ago) megafauna continued to survive.

Ventana Cave, a cave in the rocks west of Tucson, Arizona, is typical of this period of higher temperatures, illustrating as it does the gradual transition from a society of hunters and gatherers to a partly sedentary life. The oldest layer at this site dates from 9300 to approximately 12,000 B.C., the later layers are dated around 5000 B.C. The tools of a hunting and gathering people were found here: scrapers and knives and, in the later layers, grindstones (a major innovation of that time), hardwood spears with narrow points and *atlatls*. Mats and nets made of yucca fiber, rabbit skins worked into blankets and simple clothing, charcoal and a variety of bones were also found. By about 5000 B.C. the people inhabiting Ventana Cave subsisted on seeds, roots, berries, edible tubers, insects, reptiles, birds and rabbits. These people were the first representatives of a new culture, one that knew how to utilize all of the desert resources.

The Cochise Sequence

The beginnings of a sedentary culture was apparent in other parts of the Southwest also: These cultures included the Anasazi (cliff dwellers), Hohokam (farmers) and Mongollon

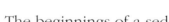

Spear points and arrow heads of basalt and flint. Left: a point from Sandia Cave (New Mexico) with a characteristic shape, MMA. Above and to the right: projectile points found in Ventana Cave (Arizona) or in other sites where Cochise Culture artifacts were found. The points are triangular and the base is narrow, making it possible to insert it into the shaft. Length: 1–2.8 inches. Early Western Archaic Period, ASM.

(who made the first bows and arrows and true pottery) peoples, whose societies began to peak around 300 B.C. The Cochise culture, also frequently referred to as the "Desert Culture," was a local variant of Archaic cultures. It developed in the Cochise country of the arid and semi-arid southeastern corner of Arizona, the southwestern corner of New Mexico, and the extreme North of what is today the Mexican state of Chihuahua. While the Cochise hunted small animals, most of their food consisted of seeds, berries and roots, a conclusion based on the fact that few projectile points have been found.

The Cochise Sequence has been divided into three periods:

The Sulphur Springs Phase (7300–6000 B.C.): The oldest *metates* and *manos* (grind-stones) found in the Southwest originated in this period, evidence that the economy was based primarily on food gathering rather than hunting.

The Chiricahua Phase (3500–1500 B.C.): This period began after a span of time for which no artifacts were found (6000–3500 B.C.). The *metate*, formerly flat, was hollowed out; stone tools consisted largely of flint knives and hammers. The well-known "split twig figurines," made of split willow twigs, originated during this period, ascribed to the simple hunting and gathering societies of the Archaic Period. The majority of these deer-like animal figurines were found in 1939 in the caves of the Grand Canyon. It is assumed that for about 1,000 years these figurines were placed in sacred caves for luck on the hunt and to obtain the goodwill of those gods who directed the course of earthly events. They are from 2.4 to 6 inches high, their size varying with the length of the cut twig. Some of these figurines are pierced by tiny spears. They are the most graceful and expressive items found among the early artistic creations of the Southwest Indians.

The San Pedro Phase (1500–500 B.C.): By this time, the climate had become wetter again. Rainfall, favorable to agricultural development, occurred more frequently. In addition to the utilization of wild plants like nuts, acorns, cactus fruit and agave roots, people began to cultivate corn, beans, pumpkins and sunflowers. This way of life allowed people to be at least partially sedentary. The first permanent dwellings, the so-called "pit houses," originated during this time, consisting of round or rectangular houses that were sunk into the ground to a depth of about 5 feet, with walls and roof formed by beams or poles covered with soil.

The Cochise people were fine basketmakers as well. They manufactured useful items such as sandals and baskets from plant fibers. They also made and used the tools essential to working with these fibers: axes, scrapers, awls, knives and other items. Simple clay pots also appeared during this period.

The oldest southwestern cultures differ little from those of other continents. Everywhere, for instance, the same techniques were used for making stone tools. Again and again men have found the same solution to a problem, reflecting mankind's great creative ability to adapt to virtually any environment.

64

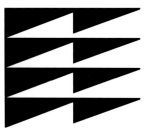 REDISCOVERY

As early as the 13th and 14th centuries many pueblos were gradually abandoned, among them Mesa Verde (in Colorado), and Chaco Canyon and Aztec (in New Mexico). Did their inhabitants migrate to a more hospitable climate? Did they die out as a result of the great drought that began in the 13th century and has continued until today? Are the contemporary Hopis and Zunis their descendants, as they believe themselves to be? Or are they the ancestors of the few Pueblo Indians who continued their communities in New Mexico (Gran Quivira, Pecos) and who were converted to Christianity by the Spaniards?

For more than half a century the abandoned settlements disintegrated, disappearing in the sand or under the thorny undergrowth. The first to cross this semi-desert in many years were the Spaniards, conquistadors from Mexico who, at the command of their king, were searching for legendary treasures—for the seven cities of Cíbola. Besides firearms and armor, they brought with them horses, which in the 17th and 18th centuries played a major role in the territorial expansion of nomadic Indians, especially the Navajos and Apaches. The Spaniards converted the last of the Pueblos to Christianity, built churches, often on top of existing Pueblo structures, and charged the padres with the governance of the new villages.

The exploration of the Southwest proceeded in one instance from the northern Sonora Desert and southern Arizona, in the other instance along the valley of the Rio Grande. In 1539 Fray Marcos de Niza entered Arizona, coming from Mexico to search for the legendary Cíbola. His search was fruitless, but he nevertheless succeeded in inflaming the emotions of his audience by describing the riches that awaited the conquerors in the new territory. Despite enormous diversity and disappointments, expeditions continued to be undertaken at irregular intervals until 1821, when the Southwest came under Mexican rule.

Among the most famous explorations, in 1540 Governor Francisco Vásquez de Coronado led an expedition of 300 soldiers and 800 Indians. Several of his men pushed on into New Mexico and reached the territory south of Gallup. In 1598–99 Don Juan de Oñate, later governor of New Mexico, attempted to establish a settlement near the present site of Santa Fe after he attacked Acoma Pueblo with 400 men and 83 wagons. The Jesuit priest Eusebio Francisco Kino in 1694 celebrated a mass in the ruins of Casa Grande, near the present site of Phoenix, and gave the place its name, "Great House," on the basis of the great walls which remained of the ruined town. He recorded his observations, and those chronicles have provided much information important to Southwest studies.

Right: Tyuonyi, the most interesting archaeological area within Bandelier National Monument (New Mexico), named for the archaeologist Adolph F. Bandelier, who was active at the end of the last century in the Southwest. The circular pueblo at one time encompassed perhaps 400 rooms and three *kivas* (only one of which has been excavated). Some of the buildings were two stories high. Between 1100 and 1550, the population was approximately 100.

In the decades that followed, Casa Grande remained an important stopping place first for the Spaniards, and later for Mexicans and American pioneers. In 1776 an expedition led by the Franciscans Silvestre Vélez de Escalante and Francísco Atanasto Dominguez, using Santa Fe as base, reached the Mesa Verde region. The expedition made its camp a few miles from the famous ruins without finding them. The two monks were not interested in ruins; they were searching for a route west to the Pacific Ocean.

The Spanish, and after them the Mexicans, had no interest in the history of the territory they occupied; their interest lay in the material exploitation and spiritual fate of the Pueblo Indians. They paid little attention to the many abandoned villages and ruins, for their everyday life was hard and the intellectual climate of that time was far from "enlightened." They saw only traces of the Meso-American civilization in the ruins. The sites had been abandoned at some point in the past, that was obvious; the precise time or the reasons why were of no concern.

While the territory was under Mexican rule from 1821–48, the first American pioneers, hunters and traders traveled through the northern part of this country. In the 1880s adventurers from the mountains headed for the goldrush in California. When Mexico ceded the Southwest to the United States, the military undertook exploratory expeditions through the territory.

In 1869 and 1871 Major John Wesley Powell became the first to explore the Grand Canyon, starting his journey at the Green River in Wyoming. Powell not only brought together topographical and geographic information about the territories he traversed, but took a great interest in their ethnographic and archaeological significance. Hundreds of Anasazi and Fremont ruins and artifacts were documented for the first time.

In 1874 the first official United States Geological and Geographic Survey of the Southwest was undertaken. Called the Hayden Survey Expedition, it included among others the photographer William H. Jackson, who became famous under the pseudonym "Pioneer Photographer." He took the first photographs of the Mesa Verde ruins, which he called "Two-Story Houses." These photographs were widely disseminated and it is partly through them that the American public learned about the Pueblos.

The first excavations of Anasazi ruins took place in the 1880s in the Four Corners Area in New Mexico, southwestern Colorado and southern Utah. Over the next thirty years excavation progressed sporadically, but these efforts were uncoordinated and largely without scientific purpose, with the exception of the remarkable work of Adolph François Bandelier. The best artifacts were removed and the rest was ignored. The first reliable, unified attempt at a systematic excavation program was made in the 1920s when trained archaeologists took over; they were the great pioneers of Southwest archaeology. Representative of this new, scientifically oriented archaeology are Alfred Vincent Kidder, N.C. Nelson, Earl Halsted Morris, and Emil W. Haury, among others.

Left: Cedar Tree Tower and a well-preserved *kiva* on the Chapin Mesa. Because of the wide view it afforded, this tower most likely served as a watch tower. Mesa Verde National Park (Colorado).

68

The period from 1915–1950 represents the high point of Southwest archaeology: The regional prehistoric cultures came to be understood as a complex of closely related cultures. As early as the 1940s most American archaeologists specializing in the Southwest began working increasingly with the ecology, local geography and cultural identity of individual Indian tribes and communities.

An introduction into the archaeology of the Southwest would be incomplete without a catalog of the many well-known specialists who made significant contributions to the research. Foremost is Adolph François Bandelier (1840–1914), a Swiss-American, who can rightly be called the founder of American archaeology. He was born in Bern and grew up in Highland, a community of Swiss immigrants in Illinois. American anthropologist Lewis Henry Morgan was a frequent guest of the family and it was on his recommendation that Bandelier made his first journey to the Southwest. He arrived in Santa Fe in 1880, and from there he explored the valleys of the Rio Grande and Pecos Rivers. Most of his time from 1881 to 1886 was spent in Frijoles Canyon. In 1916 this area (now New Mexico) came under the protection of the American government and was named Bandelier National Monument.

This is also the site of Bandelier's novel, *Die Koshare*, originally written in German, which appeared in 1890 in English as *The Delight Makers*; it became a classic of American literature at the end of the 19th century. The novel represents the first attempt to reconstruct the daily life of a Pueblo village in the 11th and 12th centuries. The success of the book rests not only on the wealth of ethnographic and archaeological material presented and its local color, but also on an absorbing plot. The reader sees the Pueblo confronted by the power of nature, sometimes antagonistic and pitiless, at other times generous and benevolent.

Books such as *The Delight Makers* helped to make the realities of life in the Southwest and the lives of Indian people known to a broad public. At the same time, the solid groundwork was laid by scientific research. Several great archaeologists contributed to this effort, for example, Cosmos Mindeleff, who directed the excavations of Casa Grande, in Arizona, under the auspices of the Smithsonian Institution in Washington, D.C. Many other important discoveries were made accidentally. Often the discoverers were amateurs who subsequently became professional archaeologists. This was the case with the startling discovery of Cliff Palace, a Pueblo ruin at Mesa Verde, Colorado. On December 18, 1888, two cowboys, Charles Mason and Richard Wetherill, searching for stray cattle during a snow storm discovered a small city of buildings as high as three stories beneath a cliff: a cliff palace.

Four days after the discovery they began to excavate the ruins. With growing enthusiasm, the five Wetherill brothers dedicated themselves to the ancient Indian cultures. In following years they dug in hundreds of sites and collected thousands of stone artifacts. Their collection was exhibited at the 1893 World's Fair in Chicago. In 1895 Richard Wetherill discovered the magnificent ruin of Keet Seel (the Kiet Siel of the Navajo National Monument

Left: Ladle made of clay with a slightly bent handle. It is decorated with a geometric design typically found on Anasazi pottery. Length: 8.12 inches. Mesa Verde National Park (Colorado), MVM.

Right: Cliff Palace at Mesa Verde, one of the most famous Pueblo cliff dwellings. This Anasazi "city" was inhabited from 1073 to 1272. At its peak it numbered 200 rooms, 23 *kivas* and about 250 inhabitants. It was built under an overhanging cliff and is 330 feet long, 100 feet wide and 66 feet high. (See also photographs on pages 124–125.)

in Arizona). At the end of his life he was working in Chaco Canyon where, according to his wishes, he lies buried.

Mesa Verde National Park brings to mind two names: Frederick H. Chapin and Gustaf Nordenskiöld. In 1892 Chapin published the first popular book about this national park, *The Land of the Cliff Dwellers.* The Swede Nordenskiöld, who directed the first systematic excavation there, published *The Cliff Dwellers of the Mesa Verde* in 1893. His extensive collection of stone tools, ceramics and other items is today owned by the National Museum in Helsinki. Also worthy of mention is Virginia McClurg: From 1887 until 1906 she led the battle in America as well as in Europe for the protection of Mesa Verde, which was being shamelessly plundered by tourists. Pursuant to the Antiquities Act, which protects all historic and prehistoric sites in the United States, Mesa Verde was declared a national park in June of 1906, and thereby placed under federal protection.

In the 1930s the husband-wife team of Robert H. and Florence C. Lister was active in Chaco Canyon, New Mexico, where the most beautiful Pueblo ruins are found. They were preceded on this site by Victor Mindeleff, Richard Wetherill, George Pepper and Edward L. Hewett, founder of the School of American Research in Santa Fe.

Partial view of the ruins of Casas Grandes. Located in the north of present-day Mexico, this pueblo was excavated by Charles Di Peso in the '50s and '60s. Casas Grandes achieved its greatest importance between 1100 and 1300, functioning as a sort of commercial center that for several centuries was the connecting link between Meso-America and the Indian cultures of the Southwest. A number of the many artifacts recovered, among them pottery and other everyday items, are held by the Amerind Foundation, which has a museum in Dragood (Arizona), about 125 miles northwest of Casas Grandes. Photo: ASM.

Another of those most active in the Southwest was Earl Halstead Morris (1889–1956) who, in 1933–34 directed the reconstruction of the great *kiva* at the Aztec ruin also in New Mexico. He subsequently participated in further excavations at the famous Mummy Cave in Canyon de Chelly, and at Canyon del Muerto, Chaco Canyon, Betatakin, Keet Seel, Mesa Verde and others. He maintained contact with other great archaeologists of his time, including Alfred Vincent Kidder.

Kidder will always be linked with the Pecos Pueblo, east of Santa Fe. Over a period of 15 years (1915–1929) Alfred V. Kidder found more than 1,200 "mummies" and skeletons. At the 1927 Pecos Conference he presented a new systematic classification of Pueblo culture based on his archaeological work, based on stratigraphy, the study of the distribution, age, and deposition of rock strata, first used by N.C. Nelson during the excavation of the Galisteo Basin south of Santa Fe. In 1924 Kidder published *An Introduction to the Study of Southwestern Archaeology*, which has become a classic not only in the realm of southwestern archaeology but for the study of archaeology as a whole. Its merit lies in the scientific approach taken by the author, based on a systematic chronology and meticulous categorization. Kidder divided the Southwest into regions. Within each region, the ruins are listed chronologically, beginning with the pueblos of the historic period and working backwards to the prehistoric and Paleo-Indian Periods. (This procedure was later imitated in other parts of the North American continent.) Thanks to Kidder, new sites continued to be located and excavated. With the aviator Charles Lindbergh, who had just completed the first direct flight from New York to Paris (1927), Kidder took aerial photographs of the plateaus and canyons, which he had divided into zones.

Finally, one should mention Emil W. Haury's work. The Snaketown excavations in particular, located south of Phoenix, Arizona, are connected with his name. Excavation was begun at Snaketown, center of Hohokam Culture, in 1934, and continued into the 1960s. Haury's book, *The Hohokam, Desert Farmers and Craftsmen*, is still the bible for those studying this culture, which lasted from approximately 300 B.C. until about 1450 A.D.

The work done over the course of this century is both extraordinary and incomplete. In Bandelier National Monument alone there are more than 1,000 sites that have not yet been excavated. And in New Mexico, in an area comprising no more than 2.5 percent of the state, 32,000 sites have been located. In the Dolores Valley of Colorado excavations have been ongoing since 1978 as archaeologists race to complete the work before the construction of a new dam makes salvaging the sites impossible. Initially two Anasazi sites were found on these two square miles; now 1,500 sites, dating from 600 to 1000 A.D. have been identified.

Public interest in southwestern archaeology has never been greater, but increases in local populations and the multiple pressures of the modern world represent a formidable threat to the Indian past. Excavations are continuing, but they are not proceeding fast enough. All too often funds for long-term, coordinated work are lacking, and meanwhile many petroglyphs are vandalized and sites plundered despite legal protection.

Above: Sandal woven of yucca fiber. It was found at Chetro Ketl, one of the most important pueblos at Chaco Canyon (New Mexico). Length: 11.6 inches. Anasazi Culture, CCP.

Pages 72-73: Winter at Wupatki National Monument (Arizona). *Wupatki* is an Indian word meaning "great house." The entire pueblo encompassed more than 100 rooms and reached a height of three stories. The red stone used in its construction is ideal in that it is easily split into horizontal slabs. The pueblo was inhabited from 1100 to 1220 and may have housed as many as 250 to 300 people. Sinagua Culture.

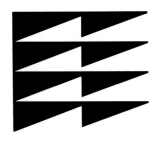

FORMATIVE CULTURAL TRADITIONS

We speak of a pre-Columbian civilization in Mexico and the societies that developed in Egypt and Sumeria as being highly developed societies, by which we mean that they reached a level of sophistication defined by a written language, a hierarchical social structure, religious temple architecture and various other features. The concept is not used in this sense with respect to the Pueblo people because they did not achieve this type of civilization. This may be largely due to their location far from any major trade route that might encourage a more active cultural exchange. It is also significant that Pueblo cultures barely reached beyond their own borders and did not transmit socio-cultural models.

American archaeologists writing about the southwestern cultures divide them into different periods and phases. With the number of collected artifacts constantly increasing, southwestern archaeology has become more detailed and complex, especially as the interrelationships and unique regional achievements unfold. This complexity is easy to understand in view of the fact that these people had to make constant adjustments to different environments, whether they were hunters, gatherers or sedentary farmers. Each culture, in addition to those attributes that were typically its own, reflected a number of borrowed characteristics and influences, which were altered over time and given new dimensions. However, nowhere in North America is there as diverse a cultural mosaic as in the Southwest, a fabric that many peoples helped to create, beginning approximately at the time of the birth of Christ and continuing until the 14th century.

After the transition from hunting and gathering to agriculture had occurred, three great spheres of activity developed in which men could exercise and hone their craftsmanship and artistic skills: architecture, pottery and rock painting. This transition occurred in the Southwest about 300 A.D. Based on this important information, scholars working between the 1930s and 1960s divided the prehistory of the Southwest into three great cultural traditions, each with characteristics typically its own: the Anasazi, the Hohokam and the Mogollon.

In order to develop a precise chronology, archaeologists rely on the minute examination of artifacts utilizing, in addition to relative chronology, new dating technologies that are absolutely accurate, such as carbon dating and dendrochronology, or tree ring dating. There are three types of cultural items: dwellings (ruins), rock paintings and artifacts. In addition to tools made of stone and bone, the artifacts include basketry (baskets, sandals and nets);

Right: One of the most impressive Anasazi ruins of the American Southwest: White House Ruin in Canyon de Chelly National Monument (Arizona). Built into the cliff between heaven and earth, "White House" owes its name in part to the whitewashed facade. It was built in 1066 and was part of a community encompassing 175 rooms and four *kivas*, which could be reached only by ladders.

animal products (furs, antlers, teeth, claws and feathers); the remains of food (animal bones, wild plant seeds, evidence of cultivated plants) and coprolites (petrified feces), well preserved in the dry Southwest climate, which, carefully analyzed, provide information about eating habits, illnesses and medical practices. Human remains, such as skeletons, teeth and hair, are counted among the artifacts and are found in graves or refuse heaps. Earl H. Morris found four well-preserved "mummies" in Mummy Cave in Canyon de Chelly, and Alfred Kidder exhumed 1,200 skeletons during his four excavations at Pecos, Texas. Finally there was the discovery of the pottery and innumerable ceramic anthropomorphic and 200 morphic figurines. The enormous variety of pottery in the Southwest shows distinct regional differences that allow archaeologists to establish a relative chronology as well as to differentiate culturally. Once again it was Kidder who first synthesized the prehistory of the Southwest, relying for his conclusions on hundreds of thousands of pot sherds collected at Pecos.

Considering that the first excavations in Europe were done in the early 19th century, archaeology on the North American continent is still comparatively young. We must also keep in mind that, especially in the Southwest, archaeologists have no written records to support their research. The ancient Indian societies had no written languages but relied on symbolic pictographs on pots and stone. The synthesis achieved at Pecos laid the foundations for the classification of archaeological cultures. The Pecos Pueblo was continuously inhabited until 1838, and Kidder was able to determine that six building complexes had been erected on the site, one after the other. The innumerable pot sherds were also extremely significant, for the pottery, which the Indian people had improved as they adapted it to their specialized daily needs, proved to be a significant indicator of each cultural change that had occurred over the centuries.

During the first Pecos Conference in 1927 the ancient cultures of the ancestors of the modern Pueblos of Arizona and New Mexico were still being divided into Basketmakers and Pueblos. Eventually it became clear that these were all the same people; what needed to be differentiated were the cultural periods. The Navajo, who migrated to the area in the 16th century, called the vanished inhabitants of the ruins "Anasazi," meaning the "ancients" or the "Ancient Enemies." Archaeologists adopted the term and it is now used to represent the entire cultural sequence.

The great archaeologists of the time participated in the first Pecos Conference: Neil Judd, who worked at Pueblo Bonito; A.E. Douglas, the inventory of dendrochronology; Frank H.H. Roberts, Earl H. Morris, Emil W. Haury, and others. Kidder used this occasion to present a chronology or timetable. His early classification of Anasazi traditions is today still considered to be largely correct. Depending on region and culture, the present state of knowledge about these cultures (discussed in detail below) has made the timetable much more complex:

Left: The roof beams (ponderosa pine) of one of the many rooms in a wall of the Aztec Pueblo (New Mexico). Because of these wooden beams, Southwest archaeologists were able to determine the year in which the trees were cut through dendrochronology (chronological determination based on annual tree rings) and thereby to establish the year in which the building was constructed.

Above: Gray, unfired anthropomorphic clay figurine. The left arm is missing. A clay "sausage" surrounds the head and the clay was slightly pinched to create the nose; the neck and hand are embellished with crosshatching; the base is rounded off. Such statuettes were placed in the ground on ceremonial occasions, particularly funerals. 2.52 × 1.76 × 0.4 inches; Fremont Culture, MNA.

77

Period	Former Designation	Current Designation
1540 – present	Historical Pueblo	Pueblo V
1300 – 1540	Regressive Pueblo	Pueblo IV
1100 – 1300	Great Pueblo	Pueblo III
900 – 1100	Developmental Pueblo	Pueblo II
700 – 900		Pueblo I
400 – 700	Modified Basketmaker	Basketmaker III
100 B.C.– 400 A.D.	Basketmaker	Basketmaker II

It was also decided at the Pecos Conference to catalog pottery according to a two-tier system based on primary site where it was discovered and its color. "Mimbres black on white," for example, means a Mimbres pot with a black pattern on a white background.

It became evident at Pecos, however, that the general classifications of 1927 were not appropriate for those archaeologists active in the Gila and Salt River basins in Arizona. The cultural traces discovered here were very different and could obviously not be found within the Anasazi tradition. Consequently other regional cultures were established, based on the discoveries made in this region: Hohokam and Mogollon. Through improvements in the dating systems used, the chronologies of these cultures have also become more precise.

The two primary methods for dating artifacts in the Southwest are carbon dating (with carbon[14]), developed by Willard F. Libby in Chicago in 1927, and dendrochronology, today used in many parts of the world. There is also thermoluminescence, which dates pottery by measuring the radioactive energy given off by a heated pottery sample; archaeomagnetic dating; and palinology, or pollen analysis, through which the environment, climate, plant and animal life of a time period can be established. The flotation technique (washing out carbonated plant remains) is also important and has become routine.

Dendrochronology, or tree ring dating, was invented by an astronomer and physicist, Andrew E. Douglas, who used this system in the Tucson, Arizona, area as early as 1913. Douglas had noted a relationship between the activity of sun spots and climatic change, which was reflected in the growth patterns of trees as indicated by the width of tree rings. A cross section of a tree trunk will show narrow and broader rings. The latter indicate years of rapid growth, therefore suggesting a damp climate; the narrow rings occur during periods of slow growth, during more or less extended dry periods. After the tree has been cut down, one looks at a cross section of the trunk, beginning at the core, and counts the rings in order to determine the age of the tree. Climatic changes that occurred during the lifetime of the tree can be determined by studying the widths of the tree rings. Examination of the cell structure within each layer makes it possible to determine even annual changes in the climate of a particular place. By overlapping a number of samples it was possible to date pines even 9000 years old. Thanks to dendrochronology, it was also possible to prove that there was an unusual period of extreme drought between 1276 and 1299. Today that

Many human and animal figurines were found in Chaco Canyon (New Mexico). While some appear to have been toys, others were clearly miniature sculptures with religious significance, which served to establish contact with the spirit world. This one is a highly stylized, if not simplified, human figure, whose facial expression is almost zoomorphic. Height: 3.2 inches. Anasazi Culture, 1100-1150 (Smithsonian Collection, Washington, D.C.), CCP.

extended drought is accepted as one plausible explanation for the disappearance or exodus of Indian people from the Four Corners Area.

Southwest Archaeology Today

By the end of the 1930s the experts were agreed: The prehistory of the Southwest was defined by three great cultural traditions—Hohokam, Mogollon and Anasazi.

Many overviews of Southwest prehistory also include other cultures, which will be briefly mentioned here. The Patayan Culture was undoubtably an independently developed culture. It is limited to the entire lower Colorado River Valley below Boulder Dam, although it spreads eastward into Arizona at the lower Gila River. Like the peoples who lived along the Nile, the Patayan lived in a narrow river valley and the annual floods washed away practically all traces of their settlement (villages, artifacts etc.). It is therefore difficult to reconstruct their culture since practically all artifacts are found on the fringes of their territory, in southeastern California, for example. The pottery clearly reflects Hohokam influence and consequently the beginning of the Patayan Culture is assumed to have been around the first century A.D. The Patayan Culture may have lasted into the 15th century and been absorbed into the cultures of the Yuma and Mohave people, but this is not certain.

Another group, the Hakataya, was named by Albert H. Schroeder and has been variously defined, even by the man who "discovered" it. In his most recent summary, Schroeder defines Hakataya as a widespread "base culture" extending from southern California well into the interior of Arizona. It therefore includes the Patayan territory and Patayan and Hakataya are often used synonymously. Also included are the small, localized cultures of the northwest plateau region of Arizona, the Sinagua and Cohonina. Schroeder also includes part of Hohokam territory (up to 500 A.D.) in the Hakataya Culture group. Since the definition of this "base culture" is ambiguous, and the chronology cannot be clearly determined, even the existence of a "Hakatayan horizon," as Schroeder once called it, is contested and for this reason the term is rarely used by most Southwest archaeologists.

The Hohokam Culture

Hohokam is a word from the language of the Pima Indians of central Arizona and means "people who have vanished." The Hohokam Culture developed in central and southern Arizona, especially at the confluence of the Gila and Salt Rivers, where water was readily available. Consequently, the Hohokam developed into the best farmers of the Southwest. Their culture is divided into four periods:

Pioneer Period (300 B.C.–600 A.D.): During this time the construction and development of Snaketown, the "capital" of the Hohokam people, took place. Large round houses

80

partially underground, often called pit houses, were built. Irrigation canals were constructed and corn, beans, pumpkin and cotton were cultivated. Ochre-colored pottery was made, either plain or decorated with simple geometric patterns (red on ochre) as well as small, anthropomorphic earthen figurines that were baked on funeral pyres. The beginning of stone work appeared and shells and turquoise were used to decorate dishes and tools and in making jewelry. The dead were cremated and their ashes buried in pits.

Colonial Period (600–900): This was a time of expansion when the culture achieved its first peak. Contact with the cultures of Meso-America intensified. Ball fields and earthen mounds for religious purposes were built; villages grew in size and number; the irrigation system was expanded. Pottery now displayed figurative as well as geometric patterns. Utilitarian and religious objects made of stone were often true miniature sculptures.

Consolidation Period (900–1100): The mounds now broadened into independent structures and formed a base for small temples and altars. The walls of the dwellings were no longer made of dried mud; the houses became massive structures made of mud or masonry supported by wooden beams. Snaketown now took up an area of about 375 acres. The pottery was decorated with complex geometric as well as theriomorphic (in the form of animals) and anthropomorphic design elements. Artifacts were now "mass produced": The craftspeople are more in evidence than the real artists. Tools and ornamentation became more versatile, but less carefully worked in their detail and shells are used extensively. The jewelry changed greatly, now consisting of shells and mosaics of turquoise and other stones. Skill and perfection of form reached their peak. Small copper bells made their first appearance, probably imported from Meso-America since copper is not a local product.

Classical Period (1100–1450): Extensive changes took place as a consequence of intensive contact with other cultures, especially the Salado and Sinagua to the northeast, both Anasazi groups. The architecture consisted of a typical "compound" surrounded by walls enclosing building complexes with varied functions, with thick walls and placed at varying distances from one another. Some of the houses are multistory, including the very impressive Casa Grande (New Mexico). The irrigation system was at its most extensive. For the first time burials in the earth are found alongside cremated remains common during the earlier periods. Red was generally used to decorate pottery and the designs were simplified. Among the tools, one now finds the adze and hoe. These new tools indicate a change in agricultural technique that is undoubtably connected with the maintenance of irrigation canals as well as the erosion of the soil.

The decline of the Hohokam Culture began around 1450. Many theories exist to explain the disappearance of these people: disease, conflict with the immigrant Salado People, invasion by the Athapaskans, changes in the climate, a long drought, collapse of those Indian cultures in Mexico with whom they carried on trade and a cultural exchange. The modern Pima and Papago Tribes are considered to be their descendants.

Spoon handle depicting a baby in a cradle. This ceramic fragment was found in the ruins at Wupatki National Monument (Arizona). Was it a decorated object for special occasions? Height: 3.2 inches. Anasazi Culture, MNA.

The Mogollon Culture

The Mogollon lived in east central Arizona and west central New Mexico, near the Mogollon Mountain Range in the middle of their territory, where most of villages are found. They developed directly out of the archaic Cochise Culture and even their early representatives cultivated corn, beans and pumpkins. The culture has been divided into several periods:

Mogollon I (300 B.C. – 400 A.D.): During this period the transition was made to permanent communities. The villages were small and consisted of several pit houses each, often including a simple *kiva* and several storage pits. The tools were made of stone and bones, bows and arrows were used and the jewelry was simple. The pottery is reddish-brown and pots were occasionally scored or incised. The dead were buried in a crouching position.

Mogollon II (400 – 600): The villages grew in size at this time. The pots were technically improved and are often two-tone (red on brown or red on white); zig-zag motifs and spirals were used as decoration.

Mogollon III (600 – 900): Agriculture was improved in various ways through the use of terraces, rows of stones or low stone walls to control erosion. The pit houses were supported by means of massive foundations and the *kivas* were larger. Like the Hohokam, the Mogollon used shells to make jewelry, but the style is simpler.

Mogollon IV (900 –1000): During this period, the population grew much larger. Influenced by the Anasazi, they built above-ground houses with masonry walls. The buildings were often several stories high and surrounded an open space. A village might consist of 200 to 300 rooms. The dead were buried under the floors. Clay pots buried with the dead were "killed" ceremonially by having a hole punched into them that, it is believed, was intended to release the spirit of the vessel so that it could join the spirit of the deceased.

Mogollon V (1000 –1200): The greatest progress in the art of pottery making was made in the Mimbres area in southwestern New Mexico. A marvelous, finely finished style of pottery came into existence here, the famous Mimbres pots. The black designs on a white background are naturalistic and abstract, their composition and originality without equal in the Southwest. In about 1100 the Mogollon lost their independence as the Anasazi colonized the northern part of their territory while the Hohokam occupied the western part.

The Anasazi Culture

The Anasazi is the best known prehistoric regional Southwest culture. Extensive sites such as Mesa Verde and Chaco Canyon have made the Anasazi much more "popular" than their immediate neighbors. It is from them that we have an incomparable legacy, especially in their architecture and crafts. Their principal territory was the southern Colorado Plateau

Page 82: Pottery from the various prehistoric cultures. From top to bottom: Left: Mug, 6.8 inches high, Pueblo Bonito, Chaco Canyon, Anasazi Culture, 1075-1150, CCP. Shallow bowl, 12.4 inches diameter, Gila River Valley, Hohokam Culture, ASM. Clay head, 1.12 inches high, Snaketown, Hohokam Culture, ASM. Middle: Polychrome vessel, Kayenta, Anasazi Culture, Navajo National Monument Museum. Coiled pot, 8.8 inches high, Chaco Canyon, Anasazi Culture, 1000-1200, CCP. Polychrome bowl, 10 inches diameter, Mogollon Culture, 1300-1400, HMP. Black-on-white bowl with "kill" hole, 8.32 inches diameter, Mimbres Valley, UCM. Right: Container from a *kiva*, 13 inches diameter, Mesa Verde, Anasazi Culture, MVM. Polychrome vessel, 6.4 inches diameter, Kinishba. Anthropomorphic jar, 5.56 inches high, Keystone Ruin, Salado Culture, ASM. Anthropomorphic vessel (polychrome), 6.2 inches high, Casas Grandes Culture (Mexico), AFM.

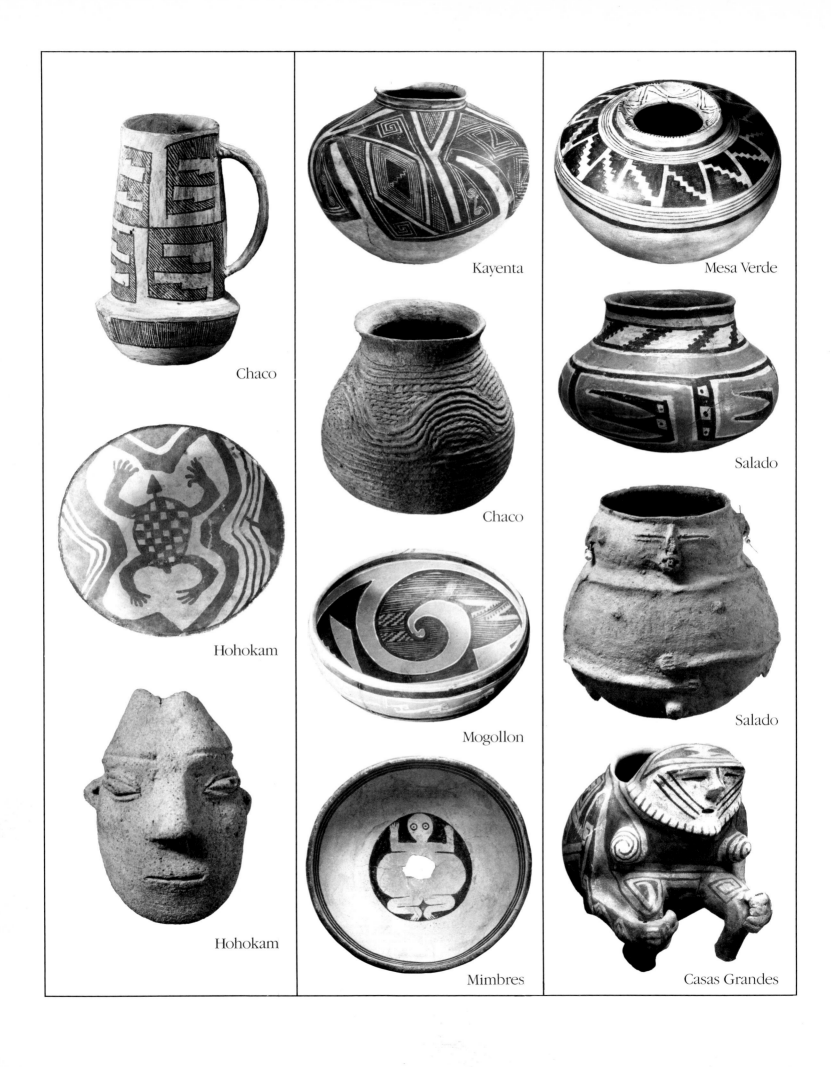

Chaco

Kayenta

Mesa Verde

Hohokam

Chaco

Salado

Mogollon

Salado

Hohokam

Mimbres

Casas Grandes

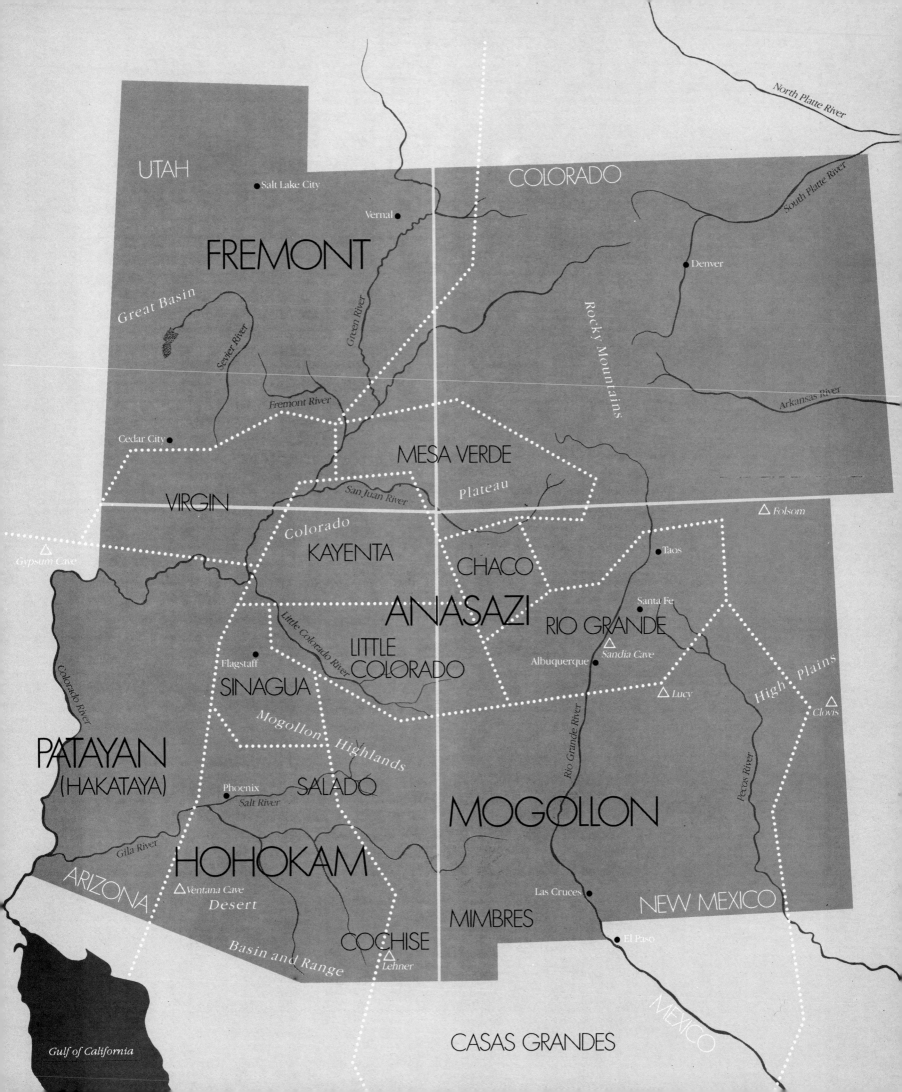

UTAH

COLORADO

• Salt Lake City

Vernal •

FREMONT

Great Basin

Green River

Sevier River

South Platte River

• Denver

Rocky Mountains

Fremont River

Cedar City •

Arkansas river

MESA VERDE

VIRGIN

San Juan River

Plateau

△ *Folsom*

Colorado

△ *Gypsum Cave*

KAYENTA

CHACO

• Taos

ANASAZI

RIO GRANDE

• Santa Fe

Little Colorado River

LITTLE
COLORADO

△ *Sandia Cave*

Flagstaff •

Albuquerque •

SINAGUA

Mogollon

Highlands

△ *Lucy*

High Plains

PATAYAN
(HAKATAYA)

Colorado River

△ *Clovis*

SALADO

Phoenix •

• Salt River

MOGOLLON

Rio Grande River

Pecos River

Gila River

HOHOKAM

ARIZONA

△ *Ventana Cave*

• Las Cruces

NEW MEXICO

Desert

MIMBRES

Basin and Range

COCHISE

MEXICO

△ *Lehner*

• El Paso

Gulf of California

CASAS GRANDES

North Platte River

between the San Juan, Little Colorado and Rio Grande Rivers. The variability in the country and its climate in part explains local differences and the Anasazi are divided into six subgroups: Rio Grande, Little Colorado, Virgin, Kayenta, Chaco and Mesa Verde. In order to simplify the discussion below, we will, however, treat the Anasazi as a cultural unity. The Anasazi Culture (which also arose from the Archaic desert culture) is divided chronologically into seven periods. A Basketmaker I period, presumed to be the oldest, is not defined in archaeological sources: When the Pecos classification system was established it was thought that artifacts from this very early period would one day be discovered.

Basketmaker II (100 B.C. – 400 A.D.): The most remarkable artifacts of this period are beautifully woven baskets, from which the group gets its name. Corn and pumpkin were cultivated. People lived in caves and built the first pit houses as well as numerous storage pits lined with upright, flat stones. The dead were "buried" in cracks or pits. Tools were made of stone or bone and people hunted with short spears thrown with the aid of an *atlatl* (a spear sling or catapult) or with darts (used for hunting rabbits). Pottery, gray and very crude, was rare and has been found only in the southernmost areas.

Basketmaker III (400 – 700): The cultivation of beans is a new feature of this group. Turkeys were domesticated and their feathers and flesh used for ceremonial purposes. Villages might consist of as many as 50 pit houses and numerous granaries and were divided into work and ceremonial areas. Bows and arrows replaced spears and *atlatls*. The pottery from this period is gray or has a black pattern on a white base.

Pueblo I (700 – 900): At this point, the communities grew in size and consisted of compact masonry houses built above ground and immediately against one another. Pit houses can still be found, but they had a new function as ceremonial houses, or *kivas*. Cotton was cultivated and products made of plant fiber became rare. The new practice of tying infants to a cradle board caused a flattening of the skull at the back of the head. In addition to simple, utilitarian pots, ceremonial pots have been found with black or red decoration against a white, red or orange colored background.

Pueblo II (900 – 1100): During this period, the Anasazi Culture achieved its widest geographic distribution. The architecture became more complex and dwellings were constructed to a height of up to five stories. The *kivas* now developed their typical form. The settlements were grouped into the canyons and on the mesas, and in Chaco Canyon they are connected by a sophisticated system of roads and steps carved into the stone. Trade relations and other contacts increased.

Pueblo III (1100 – 1300): The Anasazi Culture reached the pinnacle of its development here, including settlements in Chaco Canyon, Mesa Verde, north of the Rio Grande in New Mexico and northern Arizona. The great houses were located under the cliffs of the canyons or high on the mesas in easily defended locations. There was an active trade with Mexico, with turquoise exchanged for shells, metals and parrots, whose feathers were used in

Drawing of a petroglyph: Man with a shield decorated with the sun sign and stars. 14.4 inches. Galisteo (New Mexico).

ceremonies or for ornamentation. There is a great deal of jewelry and a wealth of pottery left from this period. The pots display diverse shapes and a new polychromy.

Pueblo IV (1300–1540): The population at this time was concentrated in several areas, mainly on the Little Colorado River and the Upper Rio Grande River Valley. Glazing was used for the first time in the pottery of the Rio Grande Valley, but only for ornamentation. Paintings of mythical and ritual scenes are found on the walls of the *kivas*. By 1450, most of the towns on the Colorado Plateau were abandoned.

Pueblo V (1540–present): During this time the Spaniards converted many of the Pueblo Indians to Christianity. Today there are 17 Pueblo communities in the Rio Grande Valley: the Acoma, Laguna and Zuni Pueblo in western New Mexico and the Hopi Pueblos in northeastern Arizona. The individual communities have different languages and socio-cultural systems, but also have many cultural elements that indicate a common ancestry.

The Fremont Culture (400 – 1300)

Named for the Fremont River, which crosses Capital Reef National Park in Utah and is spread across the Colorado Plateau and eastern Great Basin, this culture is not usually considered part of the Southwest cultural group. It is known primarily for its remarkable petroglyphs, which are clearly differentiated in style from others in the Southwest. In this and the so-called figurine-complex they differ somewhat from the Anasazi culture by which they were influenced: Local hunters encountered the permanently settled Anasazi, from whom they adopted many typically Anasazi cultural elements. Anasazi architecture (adobe houses) was copied during a late phase, but true *kivas* have not been found. The Fremont people cultivated corn and irrigated their fields, but also lived by hunting and gathering. The pottery is gray and simple; late pots were decorated with designs in black. After the Anasazi withdrew from the Colorado Plateau these formative influences—permanent settlements, cultivated crops, pottery—disappeared from the Fremont Region.

Despite all of the differences between the cultures of the Southwest, there are frequent indications of probable Meso-American influence on all of them. The exchange occurred by way of trade centers scattered across western and northern Mexico. Casas Grandes in the Chihuahua Desert, 180 miles south of the American city of El Paso, was one of these centers, possibly the most significant from the 10th to the 14th centuries. Large amounts of turquoise, shells and jet were found there. According to current information and based on the excavations made by Charles C. Di Peso between 1958 and the end of the 1960s, Casas Grandes appears to have been an important link between the highly developed civilizations of Meso-America and the Anasazi. The Hohokam–Meso-American trade, on the other hand, evolved along a corridor west of the Sierra Madre Occidental.

Pages 86-87: Turquoise fragments and turquoise jewelry. Page 86, from the top: Turquoise pendant in the shape of a "thunderbird" with a hole for a thong, .96 inches long, 2 inches thick. Snaketown, Hohokam Culture, ASM. Mosaic of a bird with spread wings, made of rectangular and square pieces of turquoise. The middle piece is reddish limestone, also in the shape of a bird, 1.78 inches long, .2 inches thick, found in a gravesite, Sinagua Culture, MNA. Pendant made with 140 turquoise pieces and an argillite piece at the center, glued to the convex surface of a sea shell, 1.88 inches long, Sinagua Culture, ASM. Page 87, from the top: Jewelry with turquoise mosaic on a sea shell, 2.18 inches. Sinagua Culture, MNA. A pair of turquoise pendants or earrings, set at the center with a red shell, 1.24 inches long and .32 inches thick, Anasazi Culture, Kayenta area, ASM. Pendant made of a sea shell set with more than 340 turquoise pieces. (See also caption for cover photograph on page 8.)

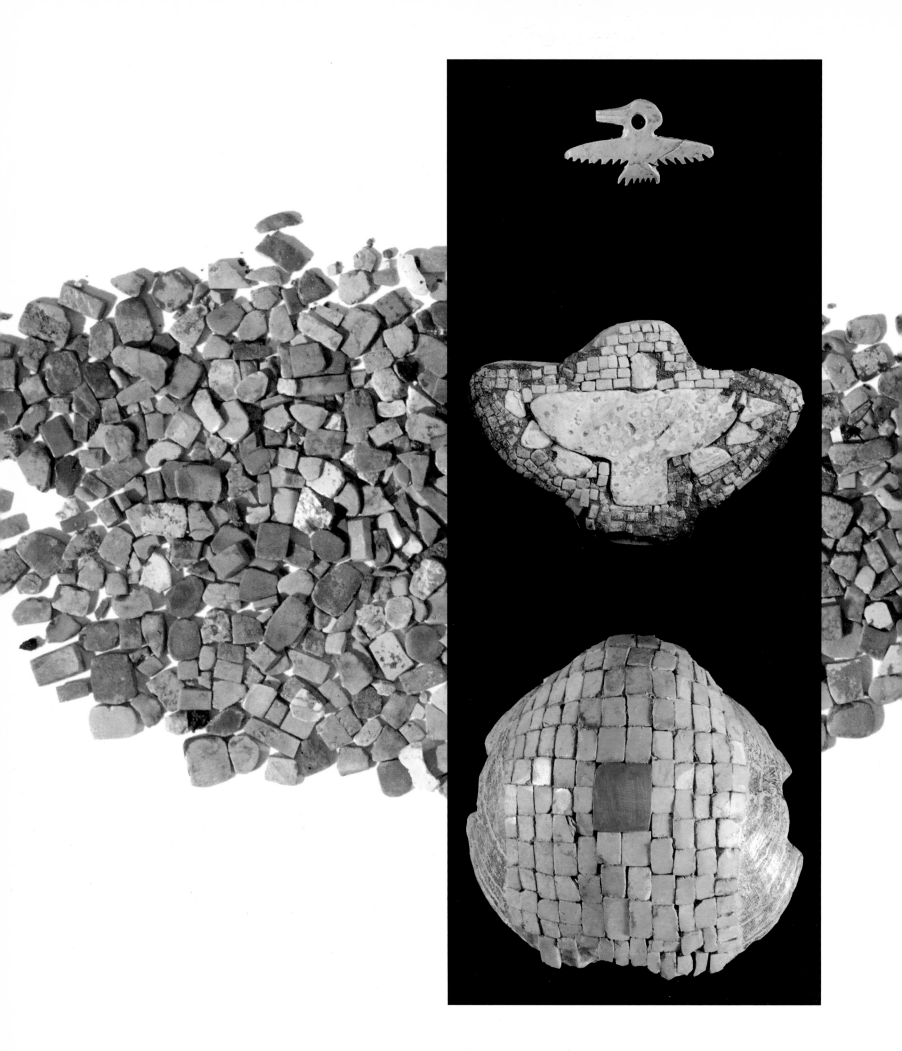

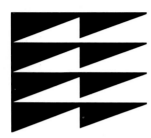

RESOURCES

At first glance nature appears harsh in the semi-arid Southwest. Closer investigation, however, shows us that she has outfitted this area with considerable wealth; one merely had to recognize and make use of it. Thanks to their extraordinary capacity to adapt and their ability to transform experience into invention, Indian people have been able to do just that. The people native to this area made use of an amazing number of natural products and established a flourishing agriculture even in the barren southwestern soil. Thanks to modern archaeological procedures (pollen analysis, etc.) and the large variety of artifacts discovered, the lifestyle of prehistoric Indian people is known to us, as are specific regional differences in the style and quality of what was produced.

Stone

Stone tools were given their optimal shape early in the Southwest and their manufacture was technologically highly developed. The prehistoric Indian people used universally known techniques such as striking, exerting pressure, hammering, grinding, polishing and drilling. Stone that was comparatively easy to work with, like flint, andecite, diorite, calcite, and quarzite, was made into spear points and arrowheads, gravedigging tools, drills, heads for axes and clubs and scrapers. The scrapers tended to be worked on both edges, with a sharp edge on one side and a blunt one on the other, and were consequently used for several tasks. Grindstones (*metates*, flat stones on which grain was ground, and *manos*, smaller stones, easily held, used to grind the grain on or in a *metate*) were made out of basalt, sandstone or limestone, as were mortars and pestles. The *manos* were made for one- or two-handed use. *Metates* came in rectangular or oval shapes and ranged from shallow basins to troughs. The modern Hopi and Zuni still use them to grind their grain and corn.

Hoes were made of sandstone. Numerous small sandstone disks have also been found. They are polished on both sides, have rounded edges, and are likely to have a hole in the center. Strung on a thong, they were worn as jewelry. On the basis of the colors and shapes of these disks it is assumed that they had religious significance. The famous balls with diameters of about 2.5 to 5 inches found everywhere in the Four Corners Area were made of sandstone, granite or flint.

Due to its rarity, obsidian was a desirable material. Tools made of obsidian were incomparably finer and sharper as well as more durable than those made of other materials.

Right: Wooden necklace or pectoral, 19.8 inches diameter, and ear pendants, 2.2 inches diameter. Found in a grave at Chetro Ketl, Chaco Canyon (New Mexico), Anasazi Culture, CCP. Part of a wooden sculpture of a parrot, 6.6 inches high, also from a grave at Chetro Ketl, Anasazi Culture, CCP.

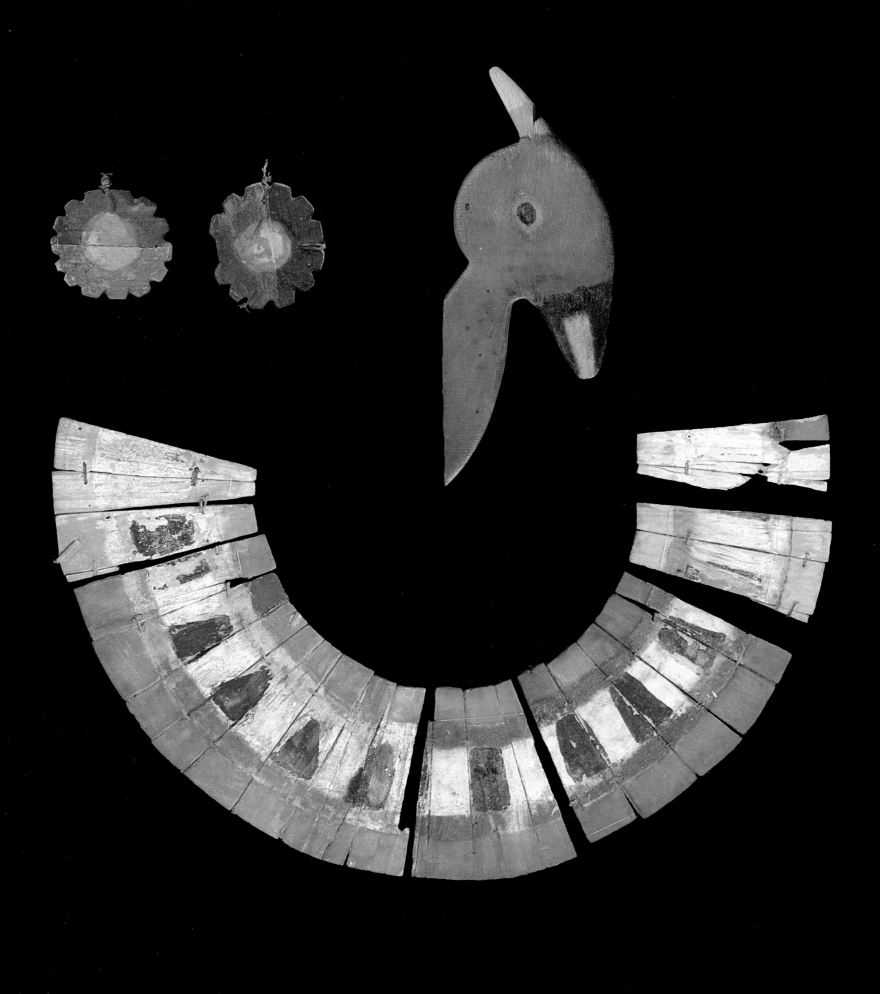

The dark, shiny lava glass came from the lava fields of the San Francisco Peaks near the modern city of Flagstaff in northern Arizona.

Shiny black jet was worn as jewelry. Other hard stones such as granite, hematite, alabaster and turquoise were painstakingly worked into polished round or cylindrical beads that were used to make necklaces. Bracelets and nose plugs were fashioned from red shale and commonly decorated with turquoise glued on with a reddish or black pitch derived from pinons, a type of pine, and other plants. This plant product was used throughout the Southwest to glue together many diverse materials to make jewelry and other items and to repair baskets, pots, etc.

Quartz crystals, mined in the Huachuca Mountains in southeastern Arizona, served as engraving tools—as indicated by their frequently worn down points—used to etch designs into rock, bone, wood and other materials. They were also used during religious ceremonies. Today the Papago use quartz crystals to prophesy and at one time the Pueblos carried them as amulets in small leather pouches. Quartz symbolized light and truth.

Hard stones such as quartzite, andecite and diorite were also used to incise pictographs. Coloring agents made of plants and minerals were used for the wall paintings: hematite for red, malachite and turquoise for green and plants for yellow.

Clay was the obvious material for making pottery and cult figurines. Stoppers and lids used to close jars and pots were made of clay also, and tubular clay pipes were used for smoking. The Anasazi were smoking tobacco introduced through Mexico as early as 700 A.D. in addition to reed "cigarettes."

Stone items of very fine quality were made by the Hohokam of quartzite, sandstone and tufa. These included drinking vessels, small pitchers and dishes used both in everyday life and for ceremonial purposes decorated with anthropomorphic and theriomorphic motifs. Those made of soapstone have a satiny smooth surface that is sensual to the touch. A thin "platter" of slate or clay, called a palette, is distinctively Hohokam. Palettes were decorated with geometric and figurative motifs representing indigenous animals and they were used in the preparation of plant and mineral pigments used for body painting.

One of the most remarkable stone creations of the Hohokam people of the Colonial Period were mirrors made of iron pyrite crystals that reflected a surprisingly sharp image. The entire surface of a round piece of sandstone, measuring about 4 to 10 inches in diameter, was covered with a mosaic of thin pyrite plates. These mirrors are proof of the level of artistic skill achieved by the Hohokam. The inlay technique and style of decoration are Meso-American in origin.

The most beautiful southwestern jewelry was made of turquoise. The Hohokam produced especially fine examples, but the Anasazi crafted fine jewelry also. Between the 10th and 14th centuries there were more than 50 turquoise mines in the Four Corners Area, most of which are exhausted today.

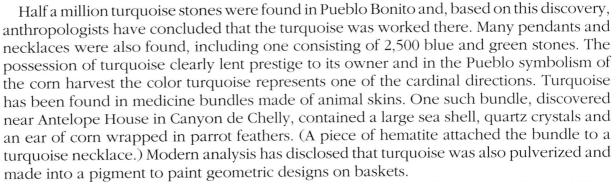

Half a million turquoise stones were found in Pueblo Bonito and, based on this discovery, anthropologists have concluded that the turquoise was worked there. Many pendants and necklaces were also found, including one consisting of 2,500 blue and green stones. The possession of turquoise clearly lent prestige to its owner and in the Pueblo symbolism of the corn harvest the color turquoise represents one of the cardinal directions. Turquoise has been found in medicine bundles made of animal skins. One such bundle, discovered near Antelope House in Canyon de Chelly, contained a large sea shell, quartz crystals and an ear of corn wrapped in parrot feathers. (A piece of hematite attached the bundle to a turquoise necklace.) Modern analysis has disclosed that turquoise was also pulverized and made into a pigment to paint geometric designs on baskets.

Raw stone was a common material also, especially rock walls and river bed pebbles. *Metates* were chipped directly into the local rock near the houses. Similarly, holes were driven into the rock to a depth of about 28 inches in order to catch and store valuable runoff during thunderstorms. Pebbles with smooth surfaces or unusual shapes were painted and thought of as lucky charms. Round stones served as cooking stones: They were heated in a fire, then lifted with wooden tongs into containers to heat water or cook food.

The Fauna

Indian people hunted deer, pronghorn antelope, rabbits, hares, foxes, peccary (pig-like animals) and many others. The Indians fished in the rivers and caught certain insects, such as grasshoppers, for food, which were ground to a fine powder and kept in storage pits. Reptiles such as the gila monster, a large lizard, and certain snakes were not eaten because they were believed to be related to the spirit of the universe. Evidence for this can be found on stylized representations (wavy and zig-zag lines) in the pictographs and carved stones found throughout the Southwest.

Hunts were conducted by pursuing the animals to the point of exhaustion, driving them over cliffs, or surrounding them. Small animals were caught in nets made of yucca fibers. Such nets could reach astonishing proportions; one found in White Dog Cave in Arizona was 240 feet long and 4 feet wide. A net woven of human hair found in New Mexico is 45 feet long.

Deerskin provided the leather for sandals, belts, thongs and clothing; the smooth tail hair was used for decoration and weaving. Antlers were made into tools and the hooves into musical instruments, particularly rattles. Bow strings, nets and thread for sewing were made of the tendons, and tools and jewelry of the bones. The stomach and bladder were used for pouches. Bits of fur decorated dresses, coats and ceremonial robes. The dead were wrapped in furs, often big-horn sheep- or deerskins decorated with feathers; rush mats held the bundle together. Belts were woven of dog hair. The museum at Mesa Verde owns one

Left and above: Tools, awls and needles of deer and bird bones. Length: from 2.86 inches. Mesa Verde (Colorado), Anasazi Culture, MVM.

Above: Two bone fragments (perhaps deer) with incisings, which may have been used in games. Each 1.12 inches long. Mesa Verde, Anasazi Culture, MVM.

of the most beautiful collections of clothing dating from the Basketmaker III Period of the Anasazi Culture, which includes a belt more than 4,950 feet long made of brown and white hair.

Because they were easy to work with, bones were used extensively by the Mogollon and Anasazi, and to a lesser degree by the Hohokam. Even in the early prehistoric time projectile points, scrapers and other items were made from the leg bones of mammoths. The most common bone tools were awls and needles. Other tools, among them knives, combs and fish hooks, were made of deer and bird bones sharpened at the ends or edges. The shoulder blades were worked into small, thin disks with diameters of 2.4 to 3.2 inches and holes in the center. They were strung alternately with brightly colored stones and shells to make necklaces. Deer teeth were also in great demand among the Fremont people, who made them into wonderful necklaces. They were so popular that those making them actually made counterfeit teeth out of bone!

Among the most remarkable and beautiful objects found in Arizona grave sites were small rods made of the polished hollow bones of large mammals. Richly decorated with spirals, zig-zag and parallel lines, they were status symbols for their owners.

As early as the ninth and 10th centuries, the Anasazi domesticated turkeys for their feathers and meat. The prayer stick, or *paho*, was made of turkey feathers. It consisted of up to 20 feathers tied together at the base with yucca fibers and fastened to an ornamental stone. They were used to decorate the altars in the *kivas* on particular ceremonial occasions, such as the corn festival, summer or winter solstice and others. According to Zuni tradition, the breeze moves the feathers and carries the words of the prayer around the circle. The feathers were also used to decorate ears of corn and for more prosaic purposes such as pillows, blankets and clothing. Turkey bones have been found in such quantities that it is assumed that flocks of these birds were kept in each Anasazi village. The Anasazi often etched or painted turkey images on stone.

Throughout the Southwest, turquoise, deer skins and other raw materials were traded for Mexican parrots, popular throughout the area for their bright yellow, scarlet, blue and copper-green feathers. Parrots were associated with religious rites. Their skeletons have been found in many graves, for instance in those of the Mimbres people, who also used stylized parrots to decorate their pottery.

The Flora

Plants were a major source of food for prehistoric Indians. The versatile ways in which these people used plants is astonishing to us, given the distance at which we live from nature. In Tularosa Cave, in a Mogollon territory of southwestern New Mexico occupied for more than 3,000 years, traces of more than 40 plants have been found here. All of them

Left: Spear points or knives of obsidian and flint, respectively. Height: 2.6 and 3 inches. Anasazi Culture, Bandelier National Monument (New Mexico).

Page 94: The yucca, one of the most important plants in the Southwest, whose parts are used for many purposes: food, clothing, tools and soap, which is made from the roots. Corrugated pot containing prehistoric yucca fiber. Diameter: 14.1 inches. Anasazi Culture (collection of E.H. Morris), UCM.

Page 95: A basket made using the coiling technique, of yucca fibers and decorated with geometric designs in red, green and yellow; the pigments were derived from minerals and plants. When the basket was discovered, it contained 48 ears of corn. Its shape is designed to facilitate transport. Height: 24 inches. Painted Cave, Lukachukai Mountains (Arizona), Anasazi Culture, AFM.

were used for food, medicine and utilitarian items. More than 60 plants discovered at sites in Arizona and Utah have been analyzed microscopically.

Nuts, acorns, berries, fruit and seeds were harvested in large quantities. They were ground and often eaten with corn meal or preserved by drying. Necklaces made of perforated acorns have been found. People ate the stalks of plants and flower stems, roots, bulbs and the tubers of wild potatoes. Various herbs were used to flavor the food: seeds, *Alopecurus* (love-lies-bleeding) and the leaves of goosefoot, a weed-like plant with green flowers, which tastes somewhat like spinach. The most commonly gathered food was pine nuts (*Pinus edulis*), rich in oil and protein. They were eaten crushed as a mush or a thick soup, or were roasted over flames until the shell cracked open and the kernel could be eaten. The pitch of this plant was ideally suited for sealing baskets, important in the days before pottery came into use in the Basketmaker II and III periods.

Another universally useful plant was the mesquite tree with its pods of nourishing seeds. The kernels were ground into meal, which was then baked into "bread." The sweet sap was used to make cakes. The Indian people made conserves, jellies and a weak alcoholic beverage out of numerous herbs and other plants. They even used plants that seem quite uninviting, such as agave, whose stems, fleshy leaves and roots were steamed in clay ovens. The flowers, buds and fruit of most cacti were eaten either fresh, dried or roasted, ground into a powder and preserved or used as a sweetener. Prickly pear (*Opuntia*) fruit was cooked into a jelly or sun dried. The tallest and most impressive Southwest cactus, the saguaro, was and continues to be an essential source of food. Even today its fruit is eaten fresh by the Pima and Papago Indians and as a dry cake soaked in a fruit syrup. Pigments

Above: Leather sandals with straps; Anasazi Culture, MVM.

Right: Woven sandals made of yucca fiber. The sandal to the left is made with a more refined technique, from Mummy Cave, Canyon del Muerto in Canyon de Chelly (Arizona). The sandal on the right is from Long House, Mesa Verde National Park (Colorado). Both Anasazi Culture, MVM.

Page 98 from top left: Bracelet made of yucca fiber and set with more than 100 turquoise pieces. Length: 4 inches. Ceremonial Cave, El Paso (Texas), Basketmaker phase of the Anasazi Culture, ASM. Bottom: A coiled basket with black geometric pattern. Diameter: 8.4 inches, Sinagua Culture, MNA. Right: Cradle made of willow rods held together with yucca fiber. At one end is a piece of deer hide intended as a footrest. Length: 26 inches. Falls Creek Cave, north of Durango (Colorado), Basketmaker phase of the Anasazi Culture, MVM.

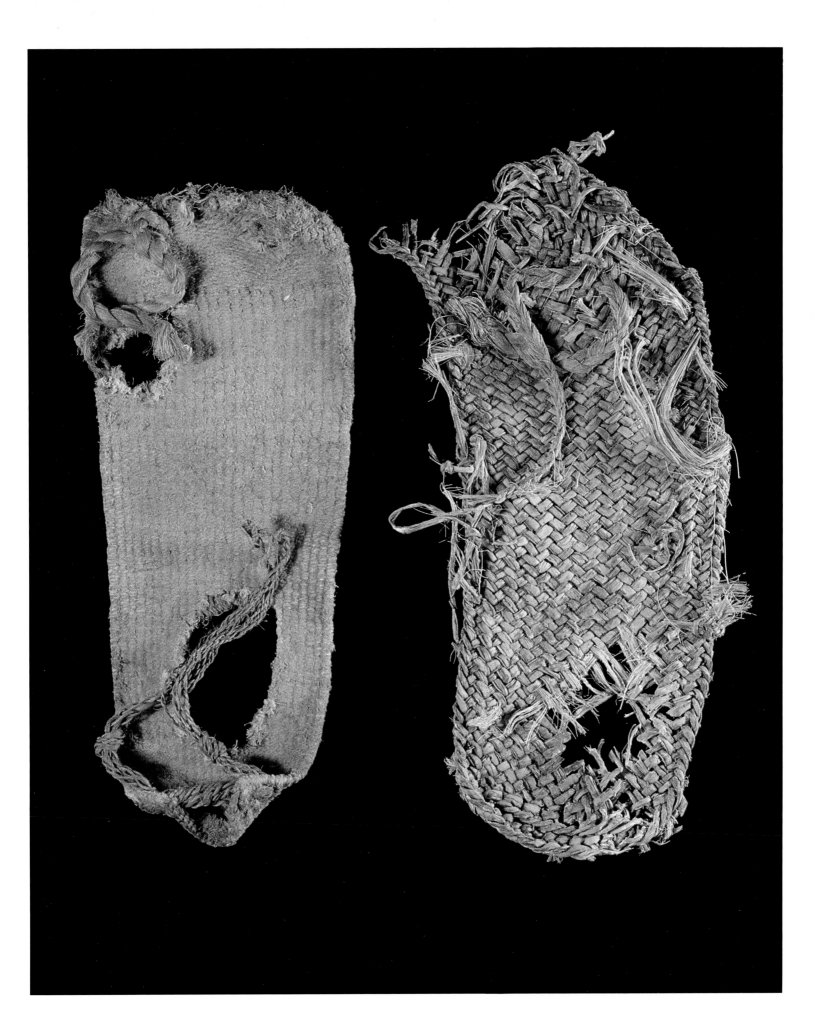

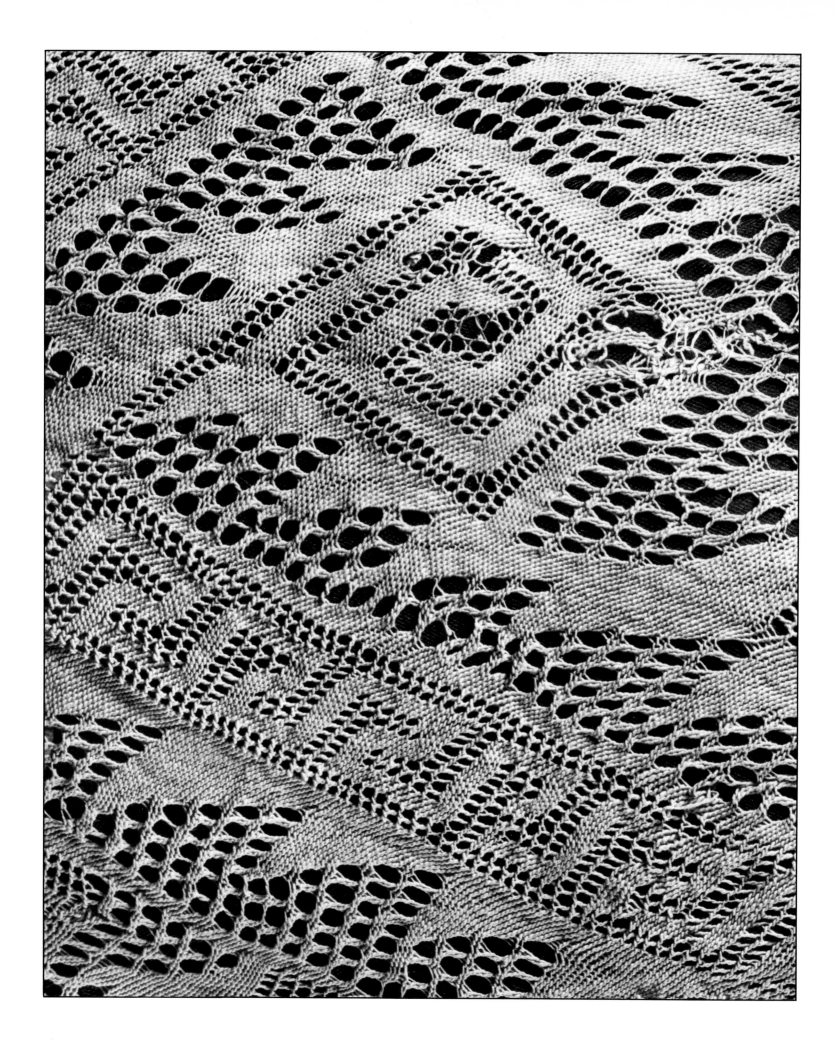

for dying clothing, baskets, blankets, leather and jewelry were extracted from various plants including lichens. The multicolored beauty of the baskets and pottery are an eloquent testimonial.

Many illnesses were cured or eased with plants. Indian people were very experienced in the art of healing and had at their disposal an abundant natural pharmacy: A concentration of juniper berries provided relief from all manner of complaints; boiled artemisia leaves were used in cases of digestive disturbances, rheumatism and colds—the Hopi still chew them today. A concentration of the Mexican cliff rose (*Cowania mexicana*) was used to cleanse wounds and promote healing. Leaves and roots were applied to bruises, sprains and burns. Bronchial complaints, fever and allergies were treated with willow bark, which contains salicylic acid, a compound that is now produced chemically; the prehistoric Indian people were already aware of the pain-reducing properties of this ingredient, aspirin.

An especially versatile Southwest plant was the yucca (*Yucca angustissima* and related species). The flowers, buds and fruit were eaten and the latter, if fermented, became a mildly alcoholic beverage. The long, narrow leaves were used to plaster the walls and ceilings of the houses. The sharp points in the leaves served as needles and the fiber was dried, crushed and cut into thin strips. The strength of the fiber made it ideally suited for basket weaving and for ropes, sandals, mats and nets. The soap made from the roots was used in purification ceremonies. Finally, fermentations derived from this plant could be used to make sparkling or mildly laxative drinks.

Corn, Pumpkin and Beans

The earliest use of corn in the Southwest is currently dated about 1000 B.C. This also takes into consideration the well-known discovery of corn in Bat Cave in New Mexico, once thought to have been 5,500 years old. Corn originally came from Mexico, where it is documented as early as the sixth century B.C. in the dry caves of the Tehuacan Valley. It actually began to play a definitive role in the development of the Southwest about 2,000 years ago, although the Hohokam may have relied on it a little earlier and the Anasazi slightly later. Corn is one of the most important factors in the development of a new agrarian lifestyle and permanent settlements. Older, small-eared varieties of corn were not especially productive and had been planted only sporadically. Between 750 and 1100, however, the Anasazi and other groups imported hardy strains from Mexico that allowed them to settle and farm in areas that were comparatively dry.

Corn was prepared in a variety of ways. The cobs were boiled in water or roasted, or the kernels were ground to meal and prepared as a gruel or porridge. It was preserved by keeping the ears in storage pits where they were protected from dampness by straw and stones.

Page 99: Left: Basket woven of yucca fiber, found in a *kiva* at Mug House, Mesa Verde National Park (Colorado), Anasazi Culture, MVM. Right: Yucca fiber, best suited for items that would get rough use such as baskets and sandals.

Left: Detail of woven cotton, one of the most beautiful examples found in the Southwest. The whole piece measures 28 × 24 inches. Tonto Cliff Dwelling (Arizona), Salado Culture, ASM.

In the rites and the symbolism of the Pueblo people corn plays an important role down to the present day. There is a Zuni saying: "Love and care for your corn as you love and care for your woman."

Two other important plants, also introduced from Mexico, were pumpkin and beans. Both can be found in general cultivation by the Hohokam, Mogollon and Anasazi about 2,000 years ago. In Bat Cave, pumpkin and beans were in evidence as well as corn. The pumpkins were stored whole or peeled and cut into strips, which were then dried and bundled. During the winter they had only to be soaked in water to regain their flavor.

Excavations of the most diverse sites have turned up several varieties of beans (*Phaseolus spp.*) dated earlier than 500 A.D. In Snaketown they were apparently introduced at the same time as corn, about 300 B.C.

Cotton

After 700 A.D. the cultivation of cotton (*Gossypium hirsutum*) spread in the Southwest. Seeds of the Mexican breed of cotton found at Snaketown have been dated to 200 A.D. In the Southwest cotton could be grown only in the low-lying areas; the elevation of the entire Colorado Plateau was too high. Cotton consequently developed rapidly into an important trade good. From around 1100, cotton blankets appear to have been woven on looms. Some of the most beautiful examples are from the Gila Basin and were made by the Hohokam. One of the truly spectacular cotton textiles was found in Snaketown, another in the ruins of the Tonto National Monument in Roosevelt, Arizona. Cotton was the most valuable trade item for the Hohokam and they carried on an active commerce in it. By 1200 the Anasazi, too, had achieved great skill in weaving cotton; their cloth sometimes has more than 325 knots per square inch.

Shells and Sea Snails

Found in variable shapes and shimmering colors, shells came from the Pacific Coast of Mexico, particularly the Gulf of California. Indian people worked on them imaginatively

Wooden comb with 10 teeth, made of sharpened willow rods and yucca fiber. Length: 5.8 inches. Shiprock, west of Aztec (New Mexico), Anasazi Culture, CCP.

and turned each shell into a small work of art. Their shell art can be favorably compared with the necklaces and bracelets produced in Europe during the Neolithic and Bronze Ages (beginning 4500 B.C.). The Mogollon and Hohokam created especially fine items: rings, bracelets, and necklaces made of variably shaped shell beads, some consisting of as many as 2,000 individual pieces, with stones and shells in an alternating pattern. One necklace consisted of 5,700 shell disks, each perforated with a stone drill! Pendants, used simultaneously as jewelry and amulets, consisted of one or two shells, carved in a geometric pattern. In later periods they were decorated with stylized animals and human shapes. Some especially beautiful pieces combine shells and turquoise in the design. The harmony of the two materials and the beauty of their colors symbolized the splendor of the world in which Indian people lived.

During the Consolidation Period of the Hohokam Culture acid engraving was discovered, a process we refer to as etching. The use of this technique in America predates its discovery in Europe by 500 years, where etching achieved its high point with German artist Albrecht Dürer in the 15th century. In Hohokam etching the surface of the object was coated with resin or pitch to seal it. The design or figure was then scraped into the coating substance with the point of a hard stone. Finally these unprotected lines were exposed to an acid, the fermented juice of the giant saguaro cactus, which ate into the surface of the shell or other object to create a design.

Water

In the dry climate of the Southwest water was a scarce resource. Indian people learned early on to dig down for water. Wells dug in 3000 B.C. were discovered near Clovis, New Mexico. As early as 2000 B.C. the Cochise people in southern Arizona dug well shafts up to 13 feet deep and 5 feet wide.

At Mesa Verde the Anasazi maintained a system of irrigation canals from 3.5 to 6.5 feet deep, many of which were lined with stones. Canals supplied water for cisterns like Mummy Lake, located on one of the mesas and used as a water supply by 950 to 1,200 people. Numerous reservoirs were also created. An entire network of canals built along the cliffs

Top: Round copper disk, divided into eight sections, with geometric designs, perhaps stylized feathers. (See detail on the following page.) The disk may have been fastened to a piece of clothing. Diameter: 9.68 inches. Casas Grandes (Mexico), AFM. Copper items reached the Southwest through trade channels starting in the 10th century. They were exchanged for pottery and turquoise and are most commonly found in Hohokam and Anasazi sites.

Above: Two wooden flutes, the mouthpieces of which have red, blue and black feathers attached with yucca fiber. The feathers came from several different southwestern birds. Length: 29.52 inches. Found in a pit house, Basketmaker III Period, Anasazi Culture, ASM.

and on the floor of Chaco Canyon caught the water from the violent summer storms, guided it over low walls, through sluices and dams into cisterns. In this way the runoff and sediment could be controlled.

The Hohokam were the irrigation specialists of the Southwest. The water supply for their highly developed agriculture was supplied by a carefully laid out system of irrigation canals. This allowed them to live at greater distances from the water, and was expanded and improved over the centuries until it could support two harvests annually. Near what is today the city of Phoenix, 240-mile-long canals have been found, which are up to about 10 feet deep, and about 30 feet wide in places. It has been calculated that it took 50 people working with wood, bone and stone tools 20 days to construct a canal measuring 3,300 feet long, 13 feet wide, and 3.3 feet deep.

Salt

Numerous salt deposits occur in the flatlands of the Southwest, east of the Rio Grande as well as along the Salt and Gila rivers of the southern region. Indian people mined the salt for their own use and for trade with Meso-America and other regions. The Anasazi of Mesa Verde thus acquired salt from the salt lakes 180 miles to the south by trading for it; the Sinagua of Walnut Canyon, Arizona, imported salt from the the Verde Valley, about 60 miles south near Montezuma Castle. Additional sources of salt (as well as shells and sea snails) were the Pacific Coast and the Gulf of Mexico.

Trade and Trading Routes

The great cultural centers at Snaketown, Chaco Canyon, Mesa Verde, Pecos and elsewhere maintained an active trade with both their immediate and more distant neighbors, including

 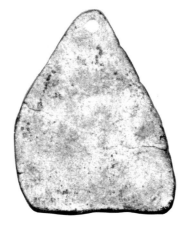 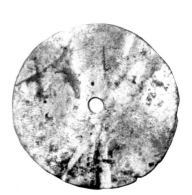

Left: Detail of the copper disk shown on page 103 in its actual size. Top: Copper container shaped like a turtle and decorated with geometric figures. Length: 4 inches, height: 1.2 inches. Casas Grandes (Mexico), AFM. Bottom: Copper axe with two holes and a haft set at 3/4 of its length. Length: 5.12 inches. Casas Grandes (Mexico), AFM.

Above from left to right: Small copper bells which were used during religious ceremonies; diameters range from 1 to 1.28 inches. Copper pendant, 2.16 inches high, weight .385 ounces. Copper disk, perhaps a pendant, 1.78 inches diameter, .02 inches thick, Casas Grandes (Mexico), AFM.

Meso-America. A complex of trails and marked roads, for instance, radiated out from Chaco Canyon. A number of so-called "traders' pouches" have been found, one of which contained more than 2,000 small shells and pieces of turquoise. The people of Mesa Verde traded their pottery, corn, pumpkins and turquoise. Popular import items from Meso-America were copper bells, about .8 to 1.2 inches in size, used during religious ceremonies. It is assumed that dancers fastened them to their belts, ankles or wrists. Hundreds have been found, mainly in Hohokam ruins. It is presumed that the trade in bells began between 900 and 1000.

This exchange of raw materials and finished products occurred along several preferred roads from the eighth to the 14th century. The oldest route led from central Mexico to Snaketown, along the western slope of the Sierra Madre, the route used by the first Spanish explorers. Another paralleled the eastern slope of the Sierra Madre and led to Casas Grandes and from there to Chaco Canyon. *Toltec* pottery fragments from Meso-America were found in Pueblo Bonito. A third important trade road connected Snaketown with the Gulf of California, crossing the Gila and the lower Colorado Rivers. It was used to trade salt and shells for turquoise and corn.

According to current scholarship, Casas Grandes played a pivotal role in connecting the great civilizations of ancient Mexico and the Southwest. Charles Di Peso, who dedicated his life to this site, was able to point out remarkable similarities in the jewelry of all these cultures; the mutual influences are undeniable. In addition to Mexican pottery, pots and other items made by the Hohokam, Mogollon and Anasazi were found at Casas Grandes; even some Fremont jewelry was uncovered. Casas Grandes was an especially important city as it was the last Mexican way station, a great trade center and marketplace. It is certain that throughout several centuries a lively exchange consisted not only of goods and food items, but also of craftspeople, who pursued their craft on both sides of today's Mexican-American border.

It is not easy to determine the significance of this exchange. We do know, however, that it is less significant than "local" trade among the southwestern cultures. Even today the tendency is to see in these indigenous cultures imported tangential manifestations of the great Meso-American cultures to the south. The artwork and crafts, however, prove that the prehistoric cultures of the Southwest soon became independent and embarked upon their own material and spiritual adventure.

Left: Ceremonial staff, a mortuary offering found in a grave in a *kiva*, carved out of the thigh bone of a grizzly bear with a precisely executed geometric design and a finely polished surface. Mogollon Culture, ASM.

Right: Shells with etched and painted animals and geometric designs. This etching technique, using cactus juice to eat away the surface, was employed in the Southwest 500 years before the technique was discovered by Europeans. Upper left: Seashell, etched with a lizard. Height: 4.12 inches. Hohokam Culture, ASM. Upper right: Shell pendant in the shape of a frog. Length: 1.64 inches. Hohokam Culture, ASM. Below: Concave inner surface of a shell with etched geometric design; the design elements are emphasized with the addition of turquoise and red pigment. Among the Hohokam pieces, this is among the most striking and beautiful. Width: 4.72 inches. ASM.

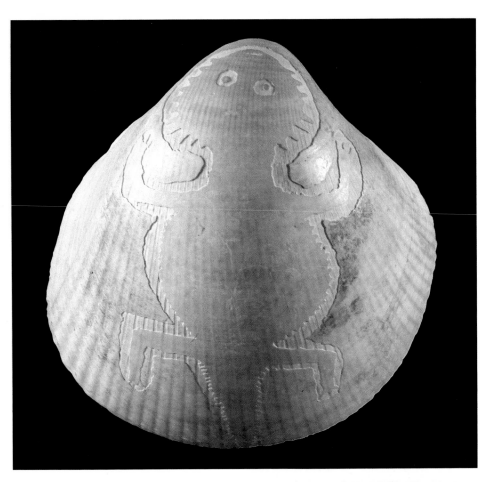

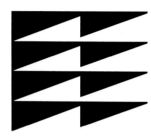

ARCHITECTURE

The first dwelling places of the Pueblo Indians were natural structures, caves or overhanging rocks and, on open land, huts made of brush, which served as temporary shelter. Caves and rock shelters such as Sandia Cave in New Mexico or Ventana Cave in Arizona were in continuous use for centuries, if not millennia.

The last century before Christ saw the beginning of permanent settlements consisting of pit houses. Often these were no more than circular or oval pits covered with horizontal timbers, supporting a layer of brush, grass and perhaps animal skins. The interior was completed by a fire pit and small storage bins dug in the walls or dirt floor. Pit houses predominated in the Southwest until approximately 700 A.D., when they were no longer built in isolation but grouped together in villages. By this time some of the communities consisted of as many as 50 dwellings.

The pit houses were clearly different from one location to another. Generally, the structures were formed in the shape of a *D*, an oval, a circle and, later, a square or even a rectangle. The diameter varied from 10 to 30 feet, and the pit could be from one to about three to five feet deep. The walls consisted of branches and brush covered with adobe. A central framework of posts and an outer circle of lighter timbers supported the roof, which was usually rounded or, less commonly, flat. The tunnel-like entrance was often located on the southeastern side. Later the entrance was moved to the side as a sort of anteroom, which over time increased in size until it became a separate room.

The pit house had one or more fire pits. An opening in the roof allowed for the circulation of fresh air and permitted smoke to escape. In later periods this opening was enlarged and, with the addition of a ladder, came to be used as the sole entrance; the former tunnel entrance became the ventilation shaft. This design was characteristic by about 600 A.D. Beginning about 700 A.D., above-ground houses became common in the Southwest, especially on the Colorado Plateau, and these were later grouped into row houses built around a plaza, creating the first above-ground villages. This building style was developed by the Anasazi, who can be called the greatest builders of North America.

This type of small village began with the settlement of Mesa Verde and consisted of a cluster of houses built in rows of varying length in either an *L* or a *U* shape. There was apparently a sort of plan, which remained fairly consistent throughout the Four Corners Area during the following centuries: Houses and storage buildings were located on the northwest side of a village; pit houses and *kivas* on the southeast side. The garbage pits

Pages 107-108: One of the great *kivas* of Pueblo Bonito, Chaco Canyon (New Mexico); 60 feet in diameter. Middle: A fire altar; these square structures, covered with boards, may have been used as floor drums, on which people danced. Jewelry and cult items were found in the square niches built into the curved walls.

Right: The long and beautiful succession of rooms on the ground floor of Pueblo Bonito, the most significant of the Southwest pueblos. The masonry attests to extraordinary building skill; the stones are so carefully fitted that mortar is superfluous. The beams protruding from the wall support the ceiling of the rooms.

were located southeast of the living areas. The village was oriented to the east, a sacred direction since that is where the sun rose. This plan was significant as it indicated a change in social organization: Villages were no longer just houses haphazardly built next to each other, but had a significant relationship with one another, accentuated by the separation of everyday living quarters from the ceremonial areas.

Since the houses were now being constructed adjacent to each other, the walls had to be built straight up and down and could no longer lean gently toward the center, as was the case with the pit houses. Initially the walls were constructed of sticks and brush rammed into the ground and then interwoven and covered over with adobe. This relatively unstable material was eventually replaced with thick tree limbs and posts. Spaces were filled in with adobe or adobe bricks, which were later augmented by stones; the term "jacal" is used to describe this type of construction. Finally, actual masonry walls were made of river pebbles and other natural stones embedded in adobe mortar. In time raw stone, trimmed to the desired shape, was used exclusively to construct masonry walls.

Permanent structures, generally rectangular in shape, appear to have been built by the Hohokam as early as 600 A.D., which is earlier than in any other part of the Southwest. This manner of construction (walls made of brush and adobe) has not changed since that time. As late as 1935 Emil Haury, an archaeologist who specialized in Hohokam culture, was able to photograph such a house constructed and inhabited by Pima Indians.

The Pueblos reached their cultural peak in the years between 1000 and 1400. During this period, real villages were erected with hundreds of rooms or in some instances—Chaco Canyon for example —large compact settlements, comparable to cities. A number of these multistory complexes consisting of numerous rooms and *kivas* were built. The building complexes were large and high—up to four stories—and were terraced. Building units were placed around a number of open areas or interior courts, or grouped around a large central plaza (in Aztec and Pueblo Bonito, for example). At this time, every pueblo could be divided into three distinct sections, containing respectively: living rooms, *kivas* and storage rooms (sometimes there are more of these than there are of living rooms). These areas could be completely independent of one another or connected by a series of passages and open-air courts.

The most impressive style of Southwestern architecture was the cliff dwelling. Often the only way to reach these structures was by means of a series of almost vertical ladders such as those found in Cliff Palace, White House, Keet Seel, Betatakin and elsewhere. Looking at one of these abandoned towns today, one is very conscious of the ingenuity, determination and technical knowledge possessed by these Indian people. Simultaneously, a number of questions arise: Why were so many buildings constructed in such inaccessible places where, moreover, there was little or no water? In some cases it was a matter of fortification, in others, these towns functioned as commercial centers. Or, perhaps people were simply better protected from inclement weather in these spaces.

Left: Examples of partially underground pit houses, the oldest permanent shelter constructed by Southwest Indian people. Made of twigs and branches covered with mud they sheltered the inhabitants from the heat in the summer and cold in the winter. Clockwise from upper left: Reconstruction of a Mogollon pit house; depth of the floor: 32 inches, Three Rivers Petroglyph Site (New Mexico). Anasazi Indian Village State Monument in Boulder (Utah). The interior of the pit house at Three Rivers Petroglyph Site. Puye Cliff ruins (New Mexico). Floor plan with post holes of a Hohokam pit house in Snaketown (Arizona). Photo: H. Teiwes, ASM.

Above: A T-shaped door with a smoke hole above it, the typical ventilation system, Walnut Canyon (Arizona).

But what about elderly people and small children? It is hard to imagine that they were able to negotiate the ladders. A careful examination of artifacts at Mesa Verde led to the conclusion that only a small fraction of the population lived in the cliff dwellings. For each cliff dwelling, there were dozens of small pueblos on the mesas, which were, by all indications, continuously inhabited into the 12th century. Perhaps the cliff houses were places of special symbolic importance during the 11th and 12th centuries when the Pueblo religion reached a ritual and ceremonial peak. Toward the end of the 11th century the Pueblo Indians began to strengthen their walls with a second layer of stones that produced a solid wall 28 inches thick. They also learned to build walls that leaned slightly inward. For the sake of stability this was a prerequisite to the construction of multiple story houses.

This perfected method of wall construction can be seen in Pueblo Bonito. Carefully shaped stones in various sizes bonded with a minimum of mortar to form a double layered wall with a center of rubble. Viewed from the outside, these walls have a completely uniform surface. Sometimes the stones are so perfectly fitted that mortar was not necessary. The roof was supported by stout pine logs with a perpendicular covering of smaller timbers and woven mats of willow branches and juniper bark. A thick layer of compacted adobe covers the entire room, forming the ceiling for the downstairs room and the floor for the one upstairs. One entered the rooms by means of ladders or through doors, which tended to be shaped like an upside-down and narrow *T*. The shape is explained by the ease with which the opening could be covered with an animal skin while leaving the lower section open for ventilation, or they were sometimes sealed with stone slabs. Forty-six of these doors were found at Mug House (Mesa Verde). The rooms were mostly small, with low ceilings, and dark, since windows were rare. This made them cool in the summer and capable of storing heat during the winter. The small size of the living spaces has given rise to the theory that the inhabitants were unusually small. However, examination of skeletons has shown that these Indians were about 5 feet, 3 inches tall, which was also the average height of humans in Europe at that time.

The walls of some of the rooms were covered with plaster decorated with paintings. Most often the designs were geometric, either isolated or grouped in rows. Common patterns were triangles, wavy lines, step-pyramids, or the stairway to heaven design, painted in white or ochre on white, such as those found at the Spruce Tree House at Mesa Verde, the Long House at Bandelier, and the Gila Cliff Dwellings. Basalt or other colored stones decorated the walls of rooms and buildings in geometric compositions that could extend into long bands. An exterior wall in the Aztec style would be embellished with a 281-foot-long band of carefully worked dark green sandstone.

The Pueblo people also built towers. Some were integrated into the houses or villages while others were connected with *kivas* by means of underground tunnels or rose from isolated but strategic places where they afforded a wide view over the country. These round,

Right: Examples of Anasazi masonry. Clockwise from the top: Wall with a dark sandstone frieze, 280 feet long, Aztec Ruins National Monument (New Mexico). The Mesa Verde style, which consists of nearly uniform stones, joined with mortar. Masonry consisting of rough stones alternating with narrow, flat slabs, creating a decorative effect, Chaco Canyon (New Mexico). A wall constructed of parallel layers of narrow stone so precisely fitted that mortar was not needed, Pueblo Bonito, Chaco Canyon.

Page 116: Access ladders, at Balcony House, Mesa Verde (Colorado); wide steps chipped out of the rock, from the floor of Chaco Canyon to the top of the cliffs; narrow footpaths worn into the soft volcanic rock through centuries of use by Indian people, at Tsankawi, Bandelier National Monument (New Mexico).

oval, *D*-shaped, square or rectangular structures appeared in southwestern Colorado (at Galena, Mesa Verde, Hovenweep) around the middle of the 11th century. Their precise purpose has not been discovered. In the case of round towers all of the stones used were contoured to form a nearly perfectly rounded shape. In some instances the walls were finished with very fine adobe that gave them a smooth, shiny appearance.

The "compound" village surrounded by a wall was introduced by the Salado people and was developed by the Hohokam. It first appeared during the classical period and remained in use until about 1450. A typical example is Casa Grande, which consists of several building complexes surrounded by a wall. The height of the walls varied from 3.3 to 23 feet. There may have been one gate or no opening in the wall at all—people entered and exited by means of ladders. Within the compound the buildings were massively built houses with walls of adobe up to 6.6 feet thick, capable of supporting several stories. Los Muertos, south of Phoenix, was another especially impressive compound. This "Village of the Dead," so-called because numerous graves were discovered there, contained 25 building complexes.

Buildings in several pueblos puzzle archaeologists: three-walled structures formed of three concentric circular walls surrounding a *kiva*. The space between the outer two walls is divided into small rooms that have no direct access to the *kiva*. Approximately 10 of these peculiar structures have been found in the Southwest, the majority of them north of the San Juan River. Best known are the Hubbard Mound at Aztec and Pueblo del Arroyo at Chaco. It is assumed that these buildings were constructed for religious purposes.

Less defined mounds—hills artificially created by heaping up earth and other materials—can also be found all over North America. They were built by different peoples at different times and served varying purposes. In the southern United States, the mounds tended to be flattened and the steps or ramps that led to the top are still visible today. Once temples, meeting halls or the houses of chieftains stood on them. The Hohokam created such pyramid-like platforms in large numbers. In Snaketown (in Arizona) alone, 60 mounts varying in height from 1 to 3.3 to 23 feet were discovered under a layer of caliche mud, a hard soil found in the Southwest. The Hohokam erected temples and altars on them.

Around 900 to 1100 the shape of the mounds underwent a transition. They assumed an oval shape, the sides were more gently sloped, their circumference tended to be around 46 feet and, based on the discovery of holes in the ground, it is assumed that the structures were supported by palisades. In the opinion of Emil Haury, only a portion of these elevated platforms served religious purposes and the majority were used for refuse disposal: Ecological problems increased in direct proportion to the height of the refuse heaps. A thousand years ago the peoples of the Southwest were already confronted by the question of waste disposal.

Above: In order to reach the cliff dwellings or to climb along the canyon walls, Indians throughout the Southwest had chipped footsize steps into the stone. This is one such a "stairway" near White House Pueblo, Canyon de Chelly (Arizona).

Pages 118-119: View of Pueblo Bonito, Chaco Canyon (New Mexico). Built between 930 and 1130, this pueblo has a diameter of 178 feet, which encompassed 800 rooms, 35 *kivas* and two great *kivas* (about 20 feet and 13 feet in diameter respectively). It was considered the largest immobile object in the world, until a larger one was created in New York in 1882. Left: Petroglyph with "stairway to heaven" or cloud pattern, both motifs commonly found in the Southwest. Using these pathways, a deceased Indian achieved heaven one step at a time. Height: 32.8 inches. Three Rivers Petroglyph Site (New Mexico).

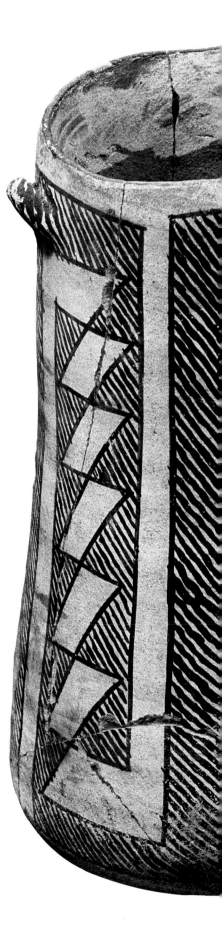

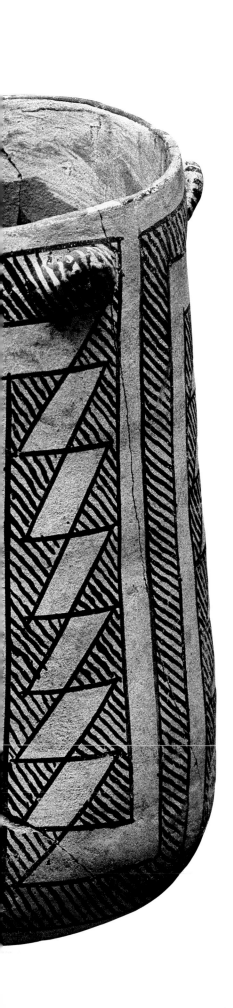

Connecting Roads

In the Chaco Canyon region a network of roads and paths encompassing more than 360 miles was discovered from aerial photographs. Constructed between 1100 and 1300, the roads lead in straight lines from the large pueblos, were planed, sometimes even stabilized with gravel, and designed without regard for topographical features. The road changed direction at sharp angles rather than curves, and these sharp turns were often edged with low walls. These roads, which were up to 30 feet wide and 60 miles long, connect dozens of communities in Chaco Canyon; some continue as far as the Aztec Pueblo. Nowhere else north of Mexico has such a highly developed network of connecting roads been found, yet we remain unsure of their use by a culture that did not use the wheel.

Additional intriguing features of Chaco Canyon are the broad steps that were chipped out of the rock and, less elaborate, the holes chipped into the rock at regular intervals. These steps led from the floor of the canyon to the rim and the plateau. The monumental stairs appear to be unique to Chaco Canyon, but the foot-size indentations are found in other ruins on the Colorado Plateau. In Tsankawi, in Bandelier National Monument, the paths are marked by narrow, deep trenches, which, through constant use, were worn into the soft, volcanic rock and polished smooth in the process. They wind in many curves from the valley to the top of the mesa.

The *Kiva*

For the modern Pueblo people, the *kiva*—a Hopi word meaning "underworld"—is a place primarily for religious activities, although it is sometimes used for secular purposes such as weaving or games. Archaeologists distinguish between small and large *kivas*, which, apart from the difference in size, are also architecturally distinct. The *kivas* developed from the original pit houses, which, as we saw earlier, became increasingly complex structures over time. The first *kivas* appear to have been constructed around the time of the birth of Christ and already displayed most of the elements characteristic of these structures.

The *kiva* is usually circular and partially underground. The Mogollon *kivas* were sometimes square. One entered through a hole in the center of the roof, the smoke hole of the early pit house. Six basic elements are common to the *kiva*, which, when the topography permits, faces south or southeast: the fire pit, which is dug into the floor or raised and made of masonry; the deflector, a perpendicular stone slab or low wall between the fire pit and the air shaft; the *sipapu*—a Hopi word meaning "navel" or "descended from"— symbol of the umbilical cord that connects Mother Earth and Indian people; and the pilasters, or masonry pillars that support the wood and adobe roof; and the bench that circled the inside wall. The roof frame consisted of several layers of crosshatched timbers, each layer fitted

Pages 120-121: Masonry at Pueblo Bonito; corner window, straight doors and T-shaped doors. Some parts of Pueblo Bonito rose to four stories. Middle: Typically cylindrical Chaco Canyon pottery, black on white, with geometric designs and four small handles at the rim. Height: 8.8 inches. 120 such pots were found in a grave at Pueblo Bonito; Anasazi Culture (Collection of the Smithsonian Institution, Washington, D.C.), CCP.

Top left: Montezuma Castle (Arizona), a cliff dwelling consisting of 20 rooms on five floors, inhabited by the Sinagua from 1100 until 1400. Ladders afforded the only access. Lower left: Montezuma Well, located within several miles of Montezuma Castle. A naturally occurring, spring fed limestone reservoir 18.5 feet deep and 158.5 feet wide. Right: irrigation canal. Above: One of the 80 towers at Hovenweep (Utah and Colorado), all built from around 1100 to 1300. This type of structure appeared largely in the northern part of Anasazi territory.

to the one below. In Mesa Verde the *kiva* of Square Tower House had eight such layers.

Some *kivas* had side tunnels that connected them with towers or underground rooms. It is unclear whether these were sanctuaries, watch towers, anterooms, or store rooms. *Kivas* were generally located in the center of a village, although they sometimes were built in remote locations where access was difficult, a detail that underscores their sacred character. One such *kiva* is Ceremonial Cave at Bandelier, located several kilometers from Pueblo Tyuonyi, high up a sheer cliff and accessible only by means of ladders.

At the peak of Anasazi culture (the Pueblo III Period, 1100–1300) great *kivas* were built, the dimensions and interiors of which exceed anything previously constructed. They generally had an entrance facing north, often with stairs. Curiously, several of these *kivas* did not have a *sipapu*. Worth specific mention are the two *kivas* at Pueblo Bonito with circumferences of 60 and 40 feet. Rectangular niches appear at regular intervals in the surrounding bench in which cult objects may at one time have been placed. Four solid stone pilasters support the roof. The fire pit, wide and rectangular, is constructed of masonry and raised off the floor. On both sides are longish depressions that served as resonance chambers for floor drums. They were covered with boards on which the priests danced. In the larger of the *kivas* the skeletons of 17 women, six children and a man were found. Buried with them were baskets, pots, stone, wood and bone tools and jewelry made of shells and turquoise.

Chaco Canyon alone has eight great *kivas*. The most striking example was found at Pueblo Rinconada, which has a diameter of 63.4 feet. Two *T*-shaped doors at opposite sides of the structure lead into a square anteroom. Did priests and dancers make their preparations there? The perfectly constructed wall is notched by 34 rectangular niches. Another great *kiva* at Chaco is at Chetro Ketl with a diameter of 55.4 feet. In its ten niches, necklaces and pendants of carved and polished stone and shells were found.

One of the most beautiful *kivas* is at Aztec Pueblo. It was reconstructed in 1934 under the direction of Earl Morris and is the only one that has been fully restored. Its diameter is 50 feet and its sheer size, combined with a majestic entrance on its north side, make it a very impressive structure. Four massive pilasters, resting on huge stone slabs, carry the 90-ton roof. They symbolize the four initiation stages through which a person must pass in order to reach the light. Surrounding the *kiva* are vertical ladders of five rungs each, leading into small chambers built into the walls. This *kiva* makes an overpowering impression. The interior space has the feeling of a church and one feels the presence of the spirit. "Entering this dimly lit room today, it is impossible not to feel its solemnity," wrote C.W. Ceram. "The carefully formed fireplace appears as altar; enclosed trenches whose significance is unknown to us look like empty sarcophagi; the square stone posts enclose the space like a church—in no other North American ruins is there so palpably the religious sense of a long vanished people as here…" (*The First American*).

Pages 124-125: Cliff Palace, Mesa Verde (Colorado), inhabited from 1073 to 1272. The "city" (110 feet long, 33 feet wide, 22 feet high) was built into a rock shelter. It is the largest cliff dwelling in America and the best known worldwide. (See also page 68.)

Left: Mummy Cave in Canyon del Muerto, one of the spectacular side canyons at Canyon de Chelly National Monument. This cliff dwelling is one of the most magnificent in northern Arizona. Many "mummies," their bodies flexed and laid on yucca mats, were found here, preserved by the dryness of the cave.

Page 128, top: Roof of a restored *kiva*, Pecos National Monument (New Mexico). The ladder at the center leads into the subterranean ceremonial room. Bottom: View into one of the *kivas* at Mug House, Mesa Verde (Colorado), with the six characteristic features: fire pit, deflector, sipapu, air shaft, pilasters and bench.

Observatories

Today it is generally accepted that the Anasazi and possibly the Hohokam built various types of "observatories," which allowed them to predict the summer and winter solstices and track the paths of the moon, stars and planets. On the basis of this information they determined the timing of religious ceremonies during the important seasons of planting and harvesting. A good harvest could, after all, be expected only when precisely timed religious rites were strictly observed. We do not know if this knowledge of astronomy was adapted from Meso-American cultures or if the Indians of the Southwest developed and practiced astronomy independently.

On a high point at Chaco Canyon called Fajada Butte, three vertical stone slabs were erected. A wide spiral etched into one of these slabs served as a sun calendar and indicated the winter and summer solstices: On the first day of summer and winter the sun's rays divide the spiral into equal halves. In the *kiva* at Casa Rinconanda, two wall niches were carved to the east and west of the north-facing entrance. At sunrise on the summer solstice the sun's rays penetrate the windows located above them in a straight line. A similar phenomenon may be observed at Pueblo Bonito in a room with corner windows. On the morning of the winter solstice the rays of the rising sun pass through these windows and fall directly on the opposite corner.

One of the most mysterious of the Anasazi constructions is the Mesa Verde Sun Temple, as it was named in 1915. A *D*-shaped structure 122 feet long and 73 feet wide, it was apparently laid out according to a design with some astronomical significance and is fascinating in the perfect symmetry of its buildings. The entire complex contains 24 rooms of various sizes, three *kivas* and a plaza. In the southwestern corner is a stone —some have called it a sundial—with four holes from which grooves radiate. When the late afternoon sunlight falls on these grooves, no shadows are formed: It is as though there were total consonance between the heaven and the earth. The Hopis call this stone the "Stone of the Sun Ray."

Should we be able to determine the full significance of these and other structures, we will have to view the Hohokam as well as the Anasazi in a new light: as cultures that were far more advanced in astronomy and mathematics than was previously supposed.

Page 129: The restored *kiva* at Kuaua, Colorado State Monument (New Mexico), is known for its beautiful 15th-century frescoes. Those shown today are copies; the originals are stored in the nearby museum. The paintings, done in black, yellow, red, blue, green and white, are related to fertility rites involving prayers for rain and the good will of the gods and the Pueblo cosmogony.

Left: The *kiva* at Aztec (New Mexico) restored by Earl H. Morris in 1934. It has a diameter greater than 16.5 feet and is proof of how carefully the builders of this "cathedral" went about their work. Monumental pillars rest on four round stone pedestals, the fire altar is raised. Around the *kiva* 14 ladders chipped into the wall lead into small round rooms. The altar is located at the north entrance, the pillars are decorated with round cedar sticks that are mortared in, of unknown, mysterious symbolism.

Above: Floor plan of the great *kiva* at Aztec (New Mexico).

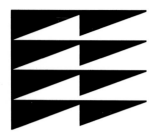 EVERYDAY LIFE

Most of the daily activities of the peoples of the Southwest were carried on in the plazas of the pueblos or on the rooftops. Assuming that the culture of prehistoric Pueblo people was similar to that of modern Pueblos, activities were gender-based. The women prepared the meals, sewed clothing, made pottery, wove baskets, tanned leather, raised vegetables, built and repaired the houses and finished the walls. They owned the houses and everything in them, even the share of the harvest that was brought home from the fields. Women were buried with the tools with which they worked during their lifetime.

Pueblo society was matrilinear, that is, descent of one's lineage was derived solely from the mother's line. A boy was a member of his mother's clan, which was different from the clan of his father. Marriage within the same clan was not permitted. The boy's mentor was his maternal uncle, whose job it was to induct the boy into the religious rites of his tribe. When a daughter married, she continued to live in the house of her mother; a room was simply added for her and her husband. When her husband died, the inheritance—such as the fields—reverted to his wife's clan. In the domestic life of this society the men were simply tolerated; their true mileu was the *kiva*, where they spent large portions of their time with comrades.

The lighting of the hearth fire was simultaneously a matter of routine and a holy act. It is likely that only designated individuals were responsible for maintenance of the hearth fire. A hardwood rod was turned very rapidly on a hardwood board until sufficient heat was generated to kindle dry grass and sawdust. Wooden fire starters such as these, with soot-blackened holes, have been found in Arizona. People came from everywhere to obtain the valuable glowing coals, as did the pioneers only a hundred years ago. Before pots and baskets were widely used, it can be presumed that food was cooked by placing it on heated stones, which were packed into leaves and covered with more hot stones.

The men hunted, fished and farmed the fields, which they owned. They helped with the construction of houses, particularly the roofs, shaped the stones, built *kivas*, wove cloth, manufactured tools of stone, wood and bones and made weapons and jewelry. The last were made either in the circle of the immediate or extended family, or else made by craftsmen who specialized in the craft. Archaeological research in Chaco Canyon has shown that, beginning around 900 A.D., specific crafts were developed at local centers. Shell and turquoise items especially appear to have been mass produced.

Pages 132-133: The pueblo of Keet Seel (or Kiet Siel), Navajo National Monument (Arizona). 115 feet long and 16.5 feet deep, it is the largest cliff dwelling in Arizona. It encompasses six *kivas* and approximately 160 rooms, 75 of which are almost perfectly preserved.

Right: The Pueblo of Betatakin, Navajo National Monument (Arizona), located a few miles southeast of Keet Seel. It contains 135 rooms and was built into a 76-foot rocky overhang within the 160-foot-high red sandstone cliff.

The cultivation and use of corn played a major role in the daily round of activities. A complex ritual was connected with this: The rising sun was formally greeted by spreading corn pollen and corn ears, stems, leaves, blossoms and flour were used in similar ceremonies. The plant was commonly represented in frescoes found in the *kivas* and in petroglyphs, carved drawings on rocks. Numerous corn dances were held during the spring, summer and fall, during planting and harvest time and when the harvest was brought in. The Hopi and Zuni people continue these traditions today.

In most parts of the Southwest corn had to be planted at least 8 inches deep to take optimal advantage of the water retained in the soil from the winter snow and spring thunderstorms. The plants were spaced about 3.3 feet from each other to permit the roots a maximum water and soil supply. Finally, pumpkin or beans were planted around the corn plants. Their foliage shaded the ground and prevented the rapid evaporation of moisture.

Since a successful harvest depended on an adequate amount of water, rain was the subject of many rites. Rattles made of hollowed-out pumpkins were imitative of the sound of falling rain; the belts of the dancers suggested upcoming rainfalls; young spruce saplings symbolized plant growth.

Only the men participated in activities requiring long treks: hunting, attacking enemies, contests of physical endurance, the carrying of news, and rituals that involved travel. At the beginning of this century the Hopis still walked up to 30 miles to work in their fields, and, like the Anasazi, they still hunted rabbits with spears. Ball fields have been found at Snaketown and Wupatki, and in many Indian legends and myths foot races play an important role. Like practically every other Pueblo activity, walking and running had highly practical value as well as cultural significance and these activities may partially explain the extensive road and trail networks that connect communities with one another.

It is known that the Pueblo Indians kept pets. Two mummified dogs were found in caves in Arizona, one buried next to its "master" and one next to its "mistress," to accompany them on their last journey. Parrots were kept for their plumage, as were turkeys, whose feathers were worked into fabric to wear as clothing. In the humorous article, "The Pueblos and the Turkey: Who Domesticated Whom?" Jean M. Pinkley playfully attempts to prove that in order to obtain turkey feathers, the Indians had no other choice than to domesticate this stubborn, fearless, highly reproductive animal.

Certainly the Indian people did not use metals, the wheel or domesticated herd or draft animals. However, were one to list the products used by the Southwestern peoples that were unknown in Europe prior to 1492, one would find among them turkeys, corn, pumpkin, cotton, sunflowers, tobacco and other cultivated plants. Their existence was simply based on criteria other than those that the ancient Europeans were accustomed to for themselves and other cultures.

Left: Bowl and *kiva* vessel: Pottery characteristic of Mesa Verde, black on white, decorated with geometric designs, creating a kinetic positive-negative effect. Diameter: 10.4 inches. The ears of corn date from the time when Mesa Verde was inhabited. Anasazi Culture, MVM.

Page 139: Three "killed" Mimbres ceramic bowls, black on white, from the Mimbres Valley (New Mexico), Mogollon Culture. Left: Stylized representation of a human figure with a club such as those used to hunt rabbits, UCM. Top: Fishing scene with nets. Next to the fisherman is a half-bird, half-human figure as guardian spirit. Diameter: 10 inches. SAR. Bottom: Representation of a man swinging a bullroarer: the faster it is swung, the higher and louder the sound produced. This instrument is still used by Pueblo people during religious ceremonies. Diameter: 7.6 inches. MMA.

Unfortunately, we know nothing about the spoken languages of early Pueblo people. The prehistoric Indian did not have a written language; we are forced to speculate whether he at least had a counting system. Did he use a type of code based, for example, on turquoise, of which numerous caches and so-called "traders' pouches" have been found? Or did he devise a practical system of communication using bundles of colored strings combined in certain meaningful ways like the Incas, another people with no written language?

Children were cherished; their graves, which were their cradles, upholstered with furs and mulched bark, are proof. Some time around 700 A.D., infants began to be strapped to a rigid cradle board during the early months of their lives. The result was a deformation of the skull characterized by a flattening of the back of the head and broad facial features— apparently desirable physical traits. When graves of the Pueblo I Period were first excavated, it was believed that a new race had appeared after the Basketmaker Period. It was not until later that the use of a cradleboard was discovered, though why they were adopted is not yet clear. Examination of skeletons and "mummies" has shown that the physical appearance of these Indians was similar to that of contemporary Pueblo people, including the Zuni and Hopi. At Mesa Verde, for instance, the men were 5 feet, 3 inches, and the women 4 feet, 11 inches tall. The body was stocky, the skull round, and the face, due to the above-mentioned deformation, broad. Skin color varied from light to dark brown, and hair color was dark brown to shiny black.

The Pueblo Indians suffered from a variety of diseases. The most frequent were arthritis, tooth cavities and abscesses, tumors, rickets, sprains and broken bones. Tooth decay appears to have been among the greatest medical problem because in the course of grinding corn a small amount of stone became mixed with the meal, rapidly wearing down the enamel. Surgical interventions were not unknown. Earl Morris found the grave of a seventeen year old girl at Aztec with a broken arm. An attempt had been made to straighten

Above: Slate pallete in the shape of a lizard; 6.8 inches long, .36 inches thick. Mortuary offering, Hohokam Culture, ASM.

Pages 140-141: Left: Jewelry of several cultures, made from sea shells and often in the shape of animals (lizards, birds, mythical monsters); Mogollon, Hohokam, Sinagua and Anasazi Cultures, ASM. Middle: Two small pendants of red shale, the upper one representing a stylized bird, the middle one a sun with a number of rays projecting from it, Pueblo Bonito, Chaco Canyon (New Mexico), CCP. Pendants made of jet with turquoise insets, Anasazi Culture, UCM. Right: Two necklaces; the smaller one with turquoise stones was found wrapped around the wrist of a child, Sinagua Culture; the longer necklace is 9.6 inches and consists of about 236 stones (one in the shape of a bird). Mogollon Culture. Noseplug of blue-green travertine. Length: 1.6 inches. Sinagua Culture, MNA.

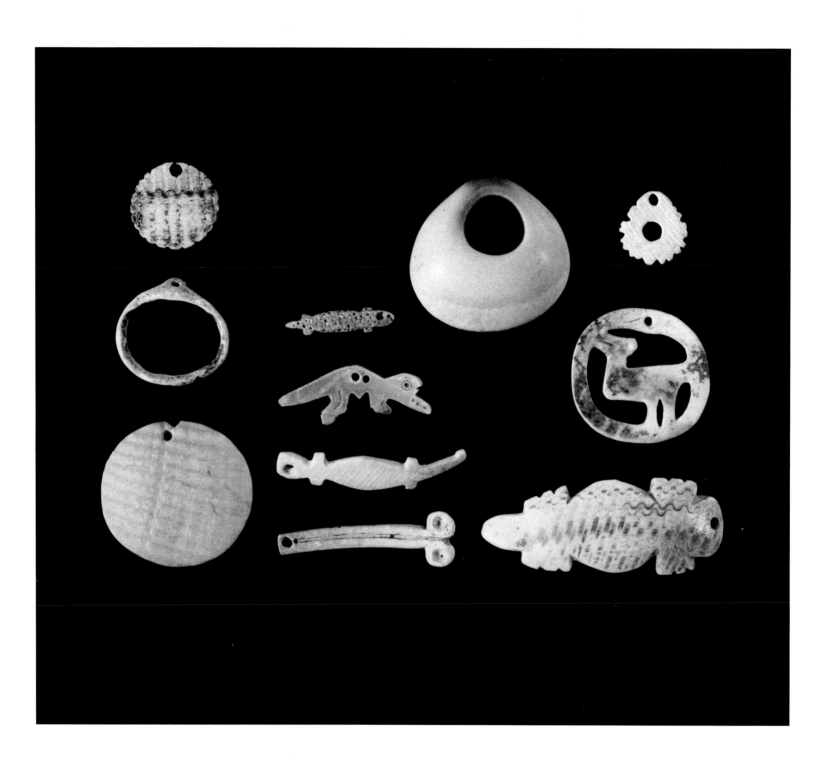

the bone by means of six slender wooden splints. Also found at Aztec was a skull that had clearly had some bone surgically removed above the left eye socket, probably with a sharp stone knife, as indicated by the smooth edges of the opening. Apparently the patient did not survive the operation.

Three activities in particular characterized all Pueblo cultures: the grinding of corn on the *metates*, of which thousands have been found; basket weaving (the beauty of these baskets is responsible for the name of the early Anasazi Periods, Basketmaker II and III); and pottery making, an art that reached its peak with the Mimbres pots and the art of the Anasazi.

The *metate*, a trough-like grindstone, is found throughout the Southwest. The term is derived from the Aztec word "metlatl." Frequently as many as three to five *metates* were found in or around a single house. The tedious work of grinding the corn was occasion for conversations among groups of women similarly engaged. Perhaps one told the legends in which corn played a symbolic role as one of the sources of life.

For several thousand years baskets have been produced by the gatherers and hunters of the Southwest, and, over a period exceeding 900 years, basketmaking developed into a fine art. Early in the Anasazi tradition (Basketmaker II Period) baskets ranged in diameter from 4 to 24 inches and storage baskets could attain a circumference of 100 inches. Often they were so tightly woven—and then coated with pitch—that they were completely watertight. It was even possible to cook in them, not over an open flame but by placing hot rocks into them.

Two techniques were commonly used: the complex coiling technique and, for larger, more loosely woven baskets, the twining method. Later, around 700 A.D., another technique came to be used, namely twilling. The shapes were quite varied, ranging from shallow trays to bowl shapes, to baskets that were deep and flared. There were also woven water baskets and conical carrying baskets with straps worn over the shoulders or forehead of the bearer to aid in the transporting of heavy loads.

Baskets were lavishly decorated in direct proportion to the refinement of basket weaving techniques. Nuances of color in the raw materials were utilized, and sometimes combined with designs in black and red and, more rarely, in green and yellow. Unique geometric designs circle the midsection of baskets in horizontal bands with a repeating pattern: zig-zag lines, triangles, a fishbone pattern, rhomboid shapes, squares, rectangles, etc.

The abstract and figurative compositions are evidence of a strongly developed sense of perspective, a total command of vaulted space and of the art of repetitive design, which never lapsed into monotony. Most impressive are the baskets, which are embellished with mosaics made of turquoise, shells and other colorful stones. A cylindrical basket was found at Pueblo Bonito the surface of which was covered with over 1,200 turquoise chips. At

Above: Pipes, used as mortuary offerings and in healing ceremonies to blow smoke over the body of the sick person. Uppermost: clay pipe; 6 inches long, Bandelier National Monument (New Mexico), Anasazi Culture, MNM. Middle and bottom: Two stone pipes, Sanders (Arizona), Anasazi Culture, MNA.

Right: Objects of clay and stone (perhaps jewelry), found largely in Hohokam burials. In the Southwest the Hohokam are considered the masters of such creations, an art characterized by its style and expressive quality. Clockwise from upper left: shallow clay bowl in the shape of a curled up snake. The incised lines represent the scaly skin; 4 inches diameter HMP. Basalt smoke maker in the shape of a big horn sheep (the horns have broken off). Length: 4.28 inches; ASM. Sandstone object in the shape of a horned toad; 8 inches diameter, ASM. Bowl carved of rhyolite with a "bas" relief of women with joined hands; 3 inches diameter, ASM. Sandstone bowl with seven frogs (water symbol); 3.76 inches diameter, ASM.

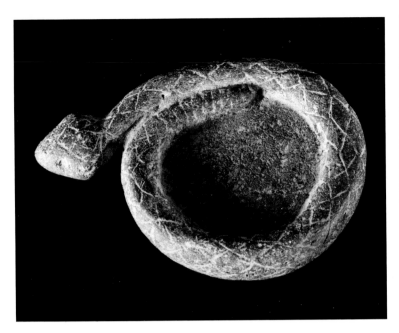

146

Ridge Ruin, near Flagstaff, a long cylindrical basket was discovered that was decorated with 1,500 pieces of turquoise, red shale and black stone as well as reddish-yellow rodent's teeth.

The making of sandals was another display of the art of weaving. The first sandals were made in the Anasazi culture around 100 A.D. and the shapes became more varied and the weaving techniques more refined until about 1000. At Aztec, Earl Morris found more than a thousand examples dated between 200 and 1200.

There were two types of sandals. One type, intended for everyday use, was quickly made from pressed yucca leaves woven over a frame of four twigs. The heel was reinforced and thongs of yucca fibers or human hair strapped the sandals to the ankle and toes. The other type of sandal, worn perhaps during ceremonies, was more carefully constructed of yucca and hemp fibers and must have taken a great deal of time to make. They were woven around a frame of 15 to 36 twigs. The sole tended to be of double thickness and the front end was angled to protect the toes. Sometimes these sandals were decorated with deerskin fringes. Around 500 A.D. people began to decorate sandals with leather at the heels and geometric designs on the sides, either painted on or interwoven. They are true works of art that reflected an increasingly sophisticated artistic development.

The Clan

Given what we have learned about the social organization of Pueblo people through the excavation of ruins, and by analogy to contemporary Pueblo societies, harmony in life depended on the ideal of merging the commonplace with spiritual, sacred activities. This combination meshed worldly and religious concerns, as two parts of a whole. The community was guided by binary, or quarterly, rhythms that joined immediate and practical concerns—hunting, farming, family life, sexuality—and transcendent religious belief. The element connecting one with the other was the clan, whose members shared a common ancestry. The man married into the family of his wife. In view of the difficult environment, which required all available physical and spiritual energy, the consensus of the group was a necessity. Social concerns and plans for collective endeavors had to be presented to a council consisting of the several heads of the clans. It is unlikely that there was a single leader, a tribal chieftain; the political system must have been dependent on the common desires of the collective.

Each clan was named after a plant, animal or natural force viewed by those belonging to the clan as a supernatural ancestor and guardian spirit: snake, lizard, turtle, lightning, etc. Perhaps the inhabitants of Chetro Ketl (Chaco Canyon) belonged to the parrot clan, for beautiful, painted, flat wooden sculptures in the shape of parrot heads were found there.

The study of architectural forms at Mesa Verde and Chaco Canyon shows that several clans may have joined together to form two groups called "moieties" by ethnologists. Each

Page 144: Top: The ball court at Wupatki (Arizona), 40 feet at its longest point. Middle: Basalt metate with mano used by the women to grind corn. Length: 17.8 inches. Snaketown, Hohokam Culture, ASM. Below left: Three stationary metates at the pueblo of Betatakin, Navajo National Monument (Arizona). Right: Depressions made in the rock by manos, near the Long House community, Mesa Verde.

Page 145: Water jug (olla), with incised lines typical of the black-on-white pottery of Mesa Verde. The thongs fastened around it are of yucca for ease of carrying. Diameter: 14.4 inches. Wetherill Mesa, Mesa Verde, MVM.

Left: Wooden club for hunting hares and rabbits. The stick is decorated with three grooves and six taut deer sinews are tied around it. It was thrown at the fleeing animal. Length: approximately 14 inches. Basketmaker II Period, Anasazi Culture, MNA.

moiety represented half of the tribe. They were geographically separated from one another by the position of *kivas* and other buildings. In competitive games (ball games) they were friendly opponents and it is supposed that they shared communal responsibilities. In the contemporary pueblos in the valley of the Rio Grande, this tradition continues as power shifts from one half of the tribe to the other twice annually, once in summer and again in winter.

Mud House in Mesa Verde is a particularly good example of this two-part division: The basic plan of the pueblo indicates the existence of two distinct areas, separated from one another by access ways. The division seems to have been based on a division of labor. The *kivas* were also divided into two groups, each group clearly having a different architectural character than the other. This plan has given rise among archaeologists to discussions about dualistic societies. One manifestation of this were the great *kivas*, which also tended to occur in pairs.

An attempt has been made to establish a hierarchy at Chaco Canyon based on significant archaeological differences in gravesites. Three levels of society have been isolated, each level perhaps assuming a specific administrative role in the system: Those with responsibility for provisions lived in the villages; the regional coordinators occupied outlying pueblos and were responsible for the harvest and the irrigation system; and the residents of the great pueblos (Pueblo Bonito, Chetro Ketl, etc.) held the central power and were the actual rulers.

Religion

For Indian people the universe is a lively place: Each stone, plant and natural force gives shape to a specific spirit. The Pueblos believed themselves to be surrounded by these spirits and sought a special relationship with them in order to win divine good will and grace. This in turn required strict adherence to and constant renewal of those rites related to important aspects of life such as hunting, seasonal change, the harvest, and rainfall. Above all, those powers that determined the course of the universe had to be placated. As was the case with other highly developed civilizations shaped by the sun, the desert, and the scarcity of water, the deities who ruled over the heaven, lightning and rain assumed the highest rank.

Top: Grooved hammer of gray porphyry; the wooden handle is held together with yucca fiber. Length: 13.4 inches. Mug House, Mesa Verde (Colorado), MVM. Below: Three-quarter grooved axe made of polished diorite. Length: 8.96 inches. Hohokam Culture, ASM.

This set of beliefs was the basis of religious life and it is through them that it becomes possible to understand the behavior of the prehistoric Indians. A hunter could not therefore despise his prey, for each animal species had its own guardian spirit who watched to see how the hunter treated the animal. A complex ritual accompanied the beginning of a hunt, the return of the hunters and the manner in which meat and bones were used and disposed of. If the hunter violated the ritual, the guardian spirit of the animal would take revenge by causing the hunter misfortune or allowing the game to become scarce. Lightning ceremonies were also repeated frequently and at regular intervals.

Religious life was centered in the *kiva*, which was the domain of the men, serving as both ceremonial and work space. Each clan maintained its own *kiva*. If no ceremonies were taking place, the men would put up their looms there, participate in meetings that determined the conduct of community affairs, and pray for the good of the whole. The initiation of a young man into the various religious practices took place in the *kiva* as soon as the boy had reached puberty. Women were permitted to enter the *kiva*, but were excluded from sacred rituals.

Kivas were led by religious leaders, the priests who guided the most important ceremonies. The large number of ceremonial chambers found in the Four Corners area is evidence that a large part of life was dedicated to religious activity. In some *kivas* have been found bone flutes and various minerals used to make body paint (red, black and white). Also discovered were quartz crystals, unusually shaped stones, animal claws, clay animals and human shapes, prayer sticks, miniature bows and pipes. Ritual practices, depending on the

Left, top: Flint projectile points, fastened to a wood shaft with animal sinew. The shaft is crudely sharpened at the end to prevent it from slipping off the *atlatl*; Basketmaker II Period, Anasazi Culture, MNA. Below: Finely worked spear and arrow points made of flint, quartz, obsidian and chalcedony. Maximum length about 3.6 inches. Snaketown (Arizona), Hohokam culture, ASM.

Above: Replica of a petroglyph (dated between 450 and 900 A.D.) representing a stylized hunting scene. The relationship between the hunter and the animal is illustrated in a direct, suggestive fashion. The work has magical as well as practical character. Exhibited at the Visitor Center at Canyon de Chelly National Monument (Arizona).

place and time, achieved a remarkable multiplicity of form that reached far back into the mythical past, into the source from which all beliefs originated. Religion not only imparted meaning to nature, but bound individuals together as a community.

First and foremost, the *kiva* was a place of consciousness between heaven and earth where the past, present and eternity merged. As E. Waters stated in *Masked Gods*, the *kiva* was a carefully recreated miniature universe. The *sipapu* led into the first underworld, the floor of the *kiva* symbolized the second world, from which the human being emerged, and the benches represented the third world. The leader led to the fourth world, in which people live today. This ancient religious world is often difficult for modern man to understand.

An important ritual item found in large numbers is the "paho," the prayer stick. A richly decorated or painted wooden stick that was jabbed into the ground, it was used by individual families as well as in the *kiva*. The bright feathers of parrots, eagles, turkeys, hawks and other colorful southwestern birds crowned the *paho* and represented the brightness of heaven and the rain-bringing clouds. Stone, wood or shell beads often gave the prayer stick a special splendor. When it was shaken, the noise mimicked rolling thunder or the tapping of rain on the hard ground. *Pahos* have been found in the *kivas* and houses (some inside the masonry), buried in the corn fields, in sacred caves, in storage rooms and in graves.

As is still the case among modern Pueblo and Navajo people, celebrations and dances were important parts of the religious ceremonies. The musical instruments, trumpets, flutes and rattles made out of gourds, turtle shells or deer hoofs, called to the guardian spirits and asked their favor. Rhythm was especially important and mirrored the complexity and regularity seen in pottery design.

Dance was particularly important in communication with the gods of thunder, lightning and rain. In *The Delight Makers*, Adolph Bandelier describes a dance scene in considerable detail, the corn dance of the Tyuonyi Pueblo, which remains one of the most sacred dances of the Hopi and Zuni. Other dances were performed in honor of particular gods, such as the snake dance. Snake pictographs appear throughout the Southwest—and it is theorized that around 1000, the same time that the trade in parrots increased, the Meso-American cult of the god Quatzalcoatl, the "feathered snake," spread into the Southwest.

Above: Drawing (based on Campbell Grant) of an *atlatl*, a weapon used by hunters since the Archaic Period (about 8000 B.C.). It measured 20 to 24 inches and consisted of a spear and a stone as weight for proper balance, allowing the spear to be thrown with much greater force. This conscious use of centrifugal force is indicative of the technical knowledge of the first prehistoric Indians. Left: Part of an *atlatl* from Canyon del Muerto, Canyon de Chelly National Monument (Arizona), UCM.

Ball Games

More than 90 ball courts found in Arizona are also indicative of significant Meso-American influences. The best known are those of Snaketown and Wupatki. The courts commonly used from 550 until 1100 A.D. were usually oval in shape; the long axis varied from 66 to 231 feet in length. In Snaketown the ball field was oriented from east to west, and at Casa Grande from north to south. There are one or two entrances at each end. The surrounding wall might have been as high as 10 feet.

The ball game was common to the people of Meso-America even before the classical period and is found in all cultures during the classical and neo-classical periods: Zapotec, Maya, Totonac, Totec and Aztec. To explain the origins of ball games the ethnologist Wolfgang Mueller has written, "The ball game appears to have been invented by Mizoque peoples during the 11th century of our time. It is related to a myth in which the sun was in danger of falling into the night and was caught by a god in the nick of time. Because the sun was so hot, he threw it to another god, who threw it to the next one. Even if this cosmic reference has been eclipsed by the later interpretation of the activity as war games, many Meso-Americans explained the sun's movement this way. In a sense to demonstrate to the sun what it should do, the mythical motion was imitated on earth."

Through the records left by early Spanish chroniclers and illustrations in the ancient Mexican manuscripts, or codices, we know how the game was played: A hard rubber ball had to be sent through a ring fastened onto a wall by the players of two teams who used knees, hips, or buttocks to propel the ball. In the neo-classical periods, the "jaguar" and "eagle" societies formed the two teams. The arc of the ball symbolized the journey of the sun. A penalty resulted if the ball touched the ground. The members of the losing team, according to stone reliefs (for example that of the great Mayan ball court of Chichén Itzá in Yucatan) were killed and their blood was offered to the gods as punishment for having interrupted the movement of the "sun," thereby endangering the world.

The Hohokam may have been familiar with this highly developed ritual ball game, but played a more "provincial" version in which no human sacrifices played a role.

Death

The manner in which the dead were buried and their graves provided with items necessary for their welfare in the hereafter were matters of great significance to the prehistoric Indians of the Southwest. Often the grave would contain a pair of new sandals, especially useful in a second life. The dead were buried in caves, in rock shelters, in sealed rooms, under

the floor, in pits formerly used for storage, and sometimes even in rubbish heaps. In the cliff dwellings themselves, however, few graves have ever been found. Children tended to be buried under the floors or inside the walls of the houses in which people lived, possibly in the belief that their souls would be reborn in subsequent generations, as the Hopi and Zuni still believed 50 years ago.

Although large gravesites have been excavated here and there (for example, more than 150 skeletons were found at Aztec), the vast majority have not been found yet, among them any cemeteries at Mesa Verde and Chaco Canyon. The remains excavated to date represent at best one one-hundredth of the erstwhile population. It is precisely the rarity of gravesites at Chaco Canyon that tends to confirm archaeologists' theories that Pueblo Bonito and other pueblos of the valley were probably religious and burial centers and the destinations of pilgrimages rather than permanent settlements.

There were two burial customs in the Southwest. The Hohokam practiced cremation. Either small pits were dug in which the corpse was burned and the ashes were left in place, or the ashes were transferred to urns, together with small clay figurines, small pots, stone tools, arrowheads, etc., and then placed into pits dug for this purpose.

Underground burials were practiced by the Mogollon and Anasazi. The dead were generally buried in a squatting position, often wrapped in a shawl or decorated blanket, and sometimes concealed inside a large basket. Later, around 1000 A.D., it became customary to bury the dead facing east, the sacred direction and symbol of rebirth, though this position was not always the rule. In the Petrified Forest and in Montezuma Cave, as well as at Mesa Verde, skeletons have been found in a flexed position with the heads toward the west or southwest. They were also found on their backs, sides or stomachs.

Some particularly puzzling archaeological discoveries include an isolated buried head, bodies without heads, a body that had been severed at the hips and then carefully sewn together again, and on a bed of grass a pair of hands and forearms with necklaces wrapped around the wrists, together with a pair of sandals decorated in black and red.

Mummified corpses dating largely from the Basketmaker II and III periods have also been found in the Southwest. They are not mummies in the usual sense of that word, however, for these peoples did not practice the embalming techniques used by the Egyptians. The bodies remained partially intact due to the combination of a dry climate and the fact that they had been buried in the furthest corner of a cave, which allowed preservation of the bodies through natural dehydration. Earl Morris examined numerous examples of these at the famous "Mummy Cave" at Canyon del Muerto. Bits of skin still adhered to the bones and bunches of hair to the scalps. Whether it was clothing, rabbit furs and sandals or *atlatls*, baskets and stone tools, on their last journey the dead were supplied with both everyday and ceremonial items. It was assumed that the same items needed in life would be required after death.

Left: Hohokam clay figurines, found at many large archaeological sites, ASM. Clockwise, from top left: Sitting person, wrapped in a sort of shawl, with turban or an unusual hairstyle. Height: 4 inches. Two ochre-colored deer. Length: 5.2 inches. Two big-horn sheep with geometric designs in red; the eyes are greatly emphasized. Height: 6.4 inches. Sitting human figure with a shallow bowl on its head; both sides of the head are painted with designs in red. Height: 5 inches.

Page 154, upper left: Clay figurine of a pregnant woman. Height: about 4 inches. Hohokam Culture, MNA. Upper right: Anasazi "mummy" wrapped in a painted cotton shawl. Painted Cave, Lukachukai Mountains (Arizona), AFM. Below: Grave of a young girl who was buried with pottery, jewelry, stone tools and sandals; around her neck is a turquoise necklace. Anasazi Indian Village, State Historical Monument (Utah).

Another important gravesite discovery was made in 1937 under the cliffs at Fall Creek, near Durango, Colorado. In addition to 17 partially mummified corpses, the body of a 22-year-old woman was discovered together with a young man. Their skeletons were completely intact. Lying between two tanned hides, they rested on mats of cedar and fir bark. The "couple" became famous under the distinctly non-Indian names of Esther and Jasper.

In 1894 the Wetherill brothers uncovered several dozen skeletons in the *kiva* of the "Sun Temple" of Mesa Verde. There was a hole in each skull as though the deceased had been killed with a hammer—perhaps in a battle or ritual killing? Earl Morris exhumed a grave at Aztec that may throw some light on the social order, which was probably headed by a priest. This grave, called the "Warrior Grave," contained the body of an extraordinarily tall man laid under a blanket of feathers and a reed mat. His upper body was covered by a large 37-by-32 inch, richly decorated, woven "shield." Among the mortuary gifts laid in his grave were beautiful stone axes. Only two other examples of such "shields" have ever been found, one at Mesa Verde and the other at Canyon de Chelly. In another site, buried next to an old man, four finely made flutes were found. Perhaps during his lifetime this old man was the ceremonial leader of a *kiva?* On the basis of new examinations of the graves found at Chaco Canyon the burial practices in Pueblo Bonito indicate the existence of a social hierarchy, glimpsed in other areas of Indian culture, though this thesis has not been finally substantiated.

From about 700 until 1200 a special practice came into use in the Hohokan and Mogollon, and especially the Mimbres, cultures. Mortuary gifts often included pottery that had a hole in the bottom. It had been symbolically "killed," setting the spirit of the pot free so that it could follow the spirit of the deceased who was usually buried underneath. This act was performed at the gravesite, as attested to by the sherds found nearby.

Pages 156–157: Mimbres pottery, black on white, Mogollon Culture. Each pot with a hole in the bottom represents a mortuary offering that was "killed," thereby setting its soul free. Upper left: The circular design shows four human figures making arrows or, according to another interpretation, playing a game. Diameter: 9 inches. MNM. Below: Bowl with a stylized bat with spread wings, one of the finest examples of representative Mimbres pottery. Diameter: 9.84 inches. ASM. Upper center: A pot in the shape of a bird with an opening at the head end. Diameter: 7.4 inches. MNA. Below: Large pot (olla) with a narrow neck and two handles, decorated with the sun symbol, stars and the stairway to heaven; MNA. Upper right: Bowl painted with a styled big-horn sheep, its body resembling a chessboard. Diameter: 9.44 inches. UCM. Below: One of the most beautiful southwestern pottery pieces, the stylized, geometric design represents two interlocking big-horn heads. It is noteworthy that this pot has not been "killed," perhaps in order to preserve the magnificent design. Diameter: 9.2 inches. MMA.

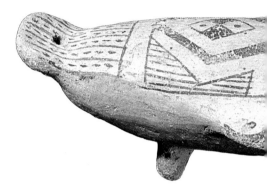

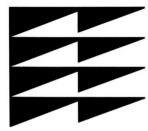 POTTERY

Today it is generally assumed that pottery making was independently invented by several cultures in the New World. There is evidence that this occurred in the Southwest as well, despite the Meso-American influence, where rudimentary sun-dried pottery pieces have been found in Basketmaker II sites. Their surfaces show traces of weaving patterns because they were formed with the aid of baskets and the clay was tempered with plant fibers. Fired briefly, these early, thick-sided pots were crudely shaped. Around the same time, another type of pottery appeared, reddish brown in color and more finely made, probably originating in Meso-America. This more advanced technique was adopted by the makers of the simple gray pottery of the Basketmaker II Period, who now began to produce a clearly superior pottery.

Apart from the early Basketmaker II pottery, the oldest ceramic ware consisted of undecorated, simply shaped, brown or red clay vessels: bowls and round pitchers. Made around 300 B.C., this pottery was found in southern Arizona and New Mexico. Despite its simplicity, this early pottery already showed considerable skill. It was not until around 500 A.D. that this advanced craft reached the northern areas of the Southwest.

Clay was readily available, found at Mesa Verde, for example, at the base of the canyons. Three types of clay were used: a dense, blue-gray clay that often made up the body of the pot; a finer porcelain clay generally used as an outer layer and for the rim; and a yellow clay that turned red in the firing process and was used for the rim or to paint on decorative patterns. The dry clay was ground to a fine powder in a *metate* and worked into a paste with water. In order to bind the clay and temper it so that it would not break during firing, shards of old broken pottery, ground to a powder, were frequently used. In this way pottery made in 1300 A.D. might contain elements of pots made centuries earlier. In other areas shiny sand, sandstone or lime, volcanic ash or pulverized sea shells were used as binding materials. Like the pottery of the Basketmaker II Period, the early pottery in other parts of the world was tempered with vegetable matter, for example, the fiber-tempered ceramics in Valdivia, Ecuador in the fourth millennium B.C.

The pigments used to glaze the pottery were derived from plants (especially in the eastern part of the Four Corners Area) and minerals (in the western part). Coal was an important source of pigment. When fired it yielded a fine black. Another source was iron, which

Right: Detail of a richly decorated Mimbres bowl, black on white. In the middle is depicted a geometric pronghorn antelope with a rhomboid head and naturalistic antlers, mouth and hooves; at its widest point the diameter is 12.32 inches. Mimbres Valley (New Mexico), Mogollon Culture, ASM.

produced a variety of colors: if fired with a large supply of oxygen, it turned yellow or gold-brown; with a low oxygen supply, the clay turned dark gray or black. In concentrated form it turned orange and red if the clay was also rich in iron.

Two techniques for molding pottery were common. One consisted of simply shaping a lump of clay by hand. The other was the coiling technique, in which bands of coiled clay were layered one on the other in spirals until the desired shape was achieved. These clay coils were then blended into a cohesive surface. The Hohokam developed the paddle and anvil technique. A lump of clay was placed on the base of an inverted, previously fired vessel or over a gourd, and then beaten. After it had dried, the pot was removed from the "mold" and the exterior was worked with a paddle while the potter held the anvil, a smooth stone, against the inside surface until the wall of the vessel was smooth and regular. Before the arrival of Europeans, the potter's wheel was unknown in America.

The number of pots collected to date runs to hundreds of thousands. Museums are overflowing with them and there are many in private collections. Institutions such as the Heard Museum in Phoenix, the Arizona State Museum in Tucson and the Museum of Indian Arts and Culture in Santa Fe own innumerable treasures. Around 1892, Earl Morris began one of the most remarkable collections of Anasazi pottery, about 400 unusual pieces, some of which are today on exhibit at the Museum of the University of Colorado at Boulder. Given the large number of pieces of pottery available in the Southwest, its variety and its stylistic development, this art serves as the standard for archaeological research and makes possible a relative chronology and classification of the various cultures.

Clay was also used for making miniature items, primarily pots ranging from 1.6 to 3.2 inches in height, which are believed to have served as toys and cult objects, created to accompany miniature human and animal figurines. Several small pots were found to contain the cremated remains of infants or small children. In the graves of the Hohokam people collections of identical animal figurines, usually deer, have been found, each figurine 2.4 to 5.2 inches long. Holes for the eyes and anus were made with a grass stem or a pointed piece of wood, and dots and an opening may represent the nostrils and mouth. These figurines, which were made for several centuries, were undoubtedly intended for fertility rituals. They were magical objects and their large number guaranteed a successful enterprise.

Hohokam Ceramics

The oldest pottery was thin walled and ochre colored, and was fired in an oxidizing atmosphere, that is, with a rich supply of oxygen. Some of the early pots were decorated

Left: Three Mimbres bowls, black on white, with stylized, naturalistic motifs; Mogollon Culture. Clockwise from left: Scorpion within a circular design representing feathers. Diameter: 10.4 inches. SAR. Two deer-like animals, one in front of the other. The tail of one covers the back of both in a composition of striking simplicity. Diameter: 10.56 inches. UCM. An animal biting its own tail, similar to the image of a coiled snake, the symbol of eternity. The naturalistic style clearly borders here onto pure geometry. 9.84 inches diameter, UCM.

Above: This clay figurine once embellished the handle of a jar or a ladle. With almond-shaped eyes, prominent nose, expressionistic in style, it is comparable to the Hohokam figurines (see photos on pages 164 and 165). Height: 2.76 inches. Mogollon Culture, ASM.

in geometric patterns in a red color. The first painted pieces appeared as early as the Pioneer Period and consisted of red or yellow patterns on an ochre background. The use of this type of painted pottery continued into the Colonial Period, although the repertoire of patterns was expanded. Common patterns were repeating elements, such as double spirals, lines and circles, as well as stylized motifs taken from nature, such as snakes and insects. One of the most popular motifs was the bird (quails, eagles or parrots), which was depicted by itself or as an element within a structured composition. Charles Avery Amsden, one of the first to thoroughly study Hohokam pottery, wrote: "The Hohokam potter is a master of the extemporaneous stroke, using her brush in truly creative delineation." In comparison with the Anasazi, "the Pueblo decorator used hers as a methodical generator of prim lines in formal geometric figures. The latter is a well-schooled draughtsman, the former an unschooled artist." Flying birds were represented by a *Z*-shape, a horizontal line or a *V*. Each piece was executed with restraint in its use of materials, the shape reduced to its

Above: The ruins of houses (occupied between 650 and 900 A.D.) and a *kiva* in the small rock shelters of Yucca Cave at Canyon de Chelly National Monument (Arizona); Basketmaker III and Pueblo I periods of the Anasazi Culture.

Right: Anasazi pottery. Clockwise from upper left: Crudely finished pot; gray, outer and inner surfaces lightly polished; 8.4 inches diameter. Kayenta Branch, ASM. Bowl, black on gray, with geometric designs (triangles with dots and crossed and zig-zag lines) on the inner surface; mortuary offering. Diameter: 7.24 inches. Wupatki National Monument (Arizona), Sinagua Culture, MNA. Pitcher with handle, black on white, with geometric designs. Height: 5.48 inches. MNA. Bowl, black on gray, with concentric lines and dots; 5.48 inches diameter, MNA. Ladle, black on white, geometric design, MNA.

essence. To quote Amsden again: "The drawing is too free and joyous to be conventional, too simple to be realistic. Perhaps simplified realism best characterizes it" (*An Analysis of Hohokam Pottery Design*, 1936).

During the Consolidation and Classical Periods the motifs became increasingly elaborate, imparting a sense of motion and refined positive-negative contrasts. There was greater variety in the shapes as well, including three- and four-footed trays, large jars with a holding capacity of nearly 26 gallons, anthropomorphic shapes, and large-bellied human figures in a sitting position with their arms resting on their knees. Soon, however, geometric patterns predominated over figurative and naturalistic representations, and the greatness of Hohokam pottery began its decline.

The making of clay figurines was an honored Hohokam tradition from the Pioneer Period to the Consolidation Period. In Snaketown alone 1,500 of them have been found, usually together with cremated remains. Whether the figures are female, male or sexually undifferentiated, they represent fertility. They were modeled by hand and often unpolished, and frequently they show the prints of thumbs or other fingers. Sometimes the arms, rumps and hairstyles are delicately formed and decorated with fine geometric lines. Some figurines consist of only a face; the rest of the body may have been made of the fibers of yucca or other plants. Perhaps the heads were once crowned with headdresses of colorful feathers. Most of the figurines were broken when they were found, leading us to wonder if they were intentionally destroyed. The discovery of isolated limbs has also given rise to the theory that some figurines had movable parts, of a type that was also produced in Meso-America.

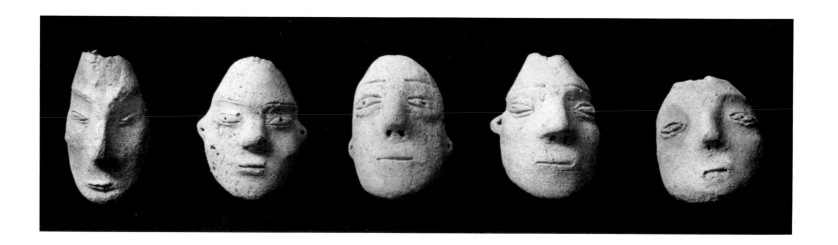

Above and facing page: A selection of clay figurines made by the Hohokam, found largely in graves. The faces are quite detailed, eyes and mouths are incised, eyelids clearly delineated. As portraits and as death masks they illustrate the transition from reality to eternity. The median length of the faces is 1.2 inches; the tallest figurine measures 3.36 inches. ASM.

Page 165, lower left: Miniature clay representation of a "forked double basket" (an object with ceremonial significance?). Height: 6.20 inches. Pueblo Bonito, Chaco Canyon (New Mexico), Anasazi Culture (Smithsonian Institution, Washington, D.C.), CCP.

Mogollon Pottery

As is the case with Hohokam pottery, the oldest Mogollon ceramic ware (plates, jars, round vessels, etc.), made around 200 B.C., was undecorated. The pieces were red, brown, even black. Beginning around 300 A.D., geometric patterns appear, painted first as broad lines, which later developed into triangles, braids, zig-zag and sawtooth lines. Red on a brown background was the predominant color combination. Between 600 and 800 it became common to use slip. Around 800, pottery with red patterns on a white background appeared and, undoubtedly as a result of Anasazi influence, so did a black-on-white coloration. This latter type eventually became the dominant style until approximately 1450.

Mimbres Pottery

A significant change in the appearance of pottery took place between 900 and 1000, the cause of which has not yet been determined: The traditional red-on-white or red-on-brown Mogollon style was supplanted by a splendid black-on-white pottery that reached its peak in southern New Mexico in the Mimbres Valley. This sudden development was undoubtedly the result of Anasazi influence. The influence of Meso-American culture is also evident, taking as its point of departure the great commercial center of Casas Grandes in northern Mexico.

These so-called Mimbres pots were decorated with geometric and naturalistic designs, the latter depicting both animals and human beings. Stylization was extensive: insects, fish, humans, birds, deer, anthropomorphic and theriomorphic (animal form) figures, the whole universe of the Southwest with always new accents in magnificent symmetrical and dynamic compositions. The execution could be incredibly fine: A band less than two inches in width, for example, may contain as many as 27 parallel lines drawn with such remarkable

Pages 166–167: Hohokam pottery with geometric and naturalistic designs. Upper left: Lid of a grave jar. Red on ochre, with rhomboids with dots in the centers. Diameter: 6 inches. HMP. Miniature pot, red on ochre, with N-shaped design. Height 3.6 inches. HMP. Left center: Three-legged pot, red on ochre, painted with a coiled snake motif, one of which is being attacked by two birds. Diameter: 4.72 inches. ASM. Deep bowl, red on ochre, painted with spirals. Height: 2.4 inches. HMP. Lower left: Deep bowl, with concentric circles and parallel lines, later repainted. Height: 2.8 inches. HMP. Pitcher found in a child's grave. Diameter: 5.2 inches. HMP. Upper center: Flat bowl, red on ochre. Diameter: 12 inches. HMP. Lower center: Shallow bowl, red on ochre, two crossed lines with quail. Diameter: 8.04 inches. ASM. Upper right: Red on ochre pot with the enlarged head and body of a seated figure. Height: 6.48 inches. ASM. Lower right: Shallow bowl, red on ochre, with a lizard or a turtle with a checkered body. Diameter: 12.4 inches; thickness: .2 inches. ASM.

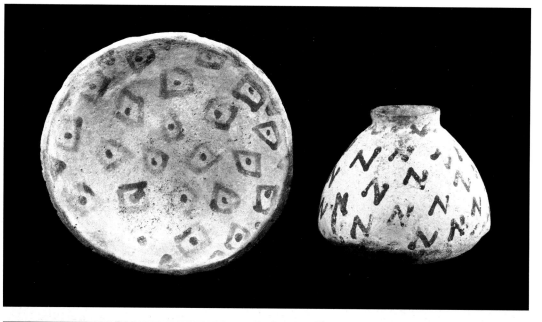

accuracy that one would suppose a special instrument had been used. There are frequent examples of the effects of perspective; fore- and background tend to be clearly separated from one another. In order to give the piece perspective and a sense of motion, distortion was used. One often finds, for example, a sort of "dagger" which, in actuality, is supposed to be a ceremonial rod. Some of the scenes in which humans and animals face each other clearly do not depict antagonistic situations but clan relationships and/or illustrations of the symbiotic relationship in which man lives with the natural world.

This pottery seems almost thoroughly modern. The shapes are daringly simple, their essence expressed in a few very pure lines. Yet the term "abstraction" does not really apply. The Mimbres potters, like the potters among other peoples in the Southwest, appear to have created realistic objects, although in a stylized form. Steven LeBlanc, a former curator of the Southwest Museum of Los Angeles, which houses a marvelous collection of Mimbres pottery, has pointed out that the Mimbres painted scenes from their daily lives. Missing, however, are plants, clothing and other utilitarian objects. On the other hand, water creatures are abundantly represented: fish, tadpoles, frogs and turtles. Since these animals had to be rather rare in the territory occupied by the Mimbres people, the designs must be understood symbolically. They communicate not so much a view of reality as an intent to call up the benign powers from the world of the spirits. The naturalist elements have transcendent aspects as well.

Archaeologists and specialists such as Jesse Walter Fewkes, the Hopi Fred Kabotie, Pat Carr, J.J. Brody and Steven LeBlanc have attempted to interpret the painted scenes on the pottery in detail by utilizing Hopi and Zuni myths and legends as well as universal archetypes. The scenes—of work, fishing, games, hunting, dances and ceremonies—are very lively and full of originality, enclosing within themselves the curved inner space of the vessel. It is indisputable that Mimbres pottery is the most beautiful in the entire Southwest and can be compared with the most spectacular creations of Meso-American and South American high cultures. In this pottery, naturalism finds its highest plastic expression. It is also interesting that the most beautiful pottery has been found in graves, that is, these pots were mortuary offerings made specifically for this purpose. Given the high quality of these wares, the question arises whether they were the work of a few potters who may have viewed their products as actual individual works of art. There is support for this idea in the repetition of identical motifs in a number of pots.

Anasazi Pottery

About 400 A.D. the pottery in use was gray and consisted of clay that was crudely bound, largely with quartz. Some of the pieces are decorated with geometric and anthropomorphic

Above: Mesa Verde pottery: two lids, black on white. Diameter: 3.64 inches. Mug House, Wetherill Mesa (Colorado), Anasazi Culture, MVM.

Right: Pottery from Casas Grandes (Mexico), Ramos polychrome, with well-executed, stylized geometric and naturalistic designs; several are anthropomorphic. The pots are painted with those design elements that were used over and over again in the Southwest, universal symbols like spirals, birds, stairways to heaven, etc. Upper left: Stylized rabbit figure. Diameter: 9.28 inches. AFM. Lower left: Square pot with four legs, painted with deer (?) and the stairway to heaven design. 3.28 inches long on a side, .12 inches thick. AFM. Upper right: Spirals and birds, with a handle in the shape of a parrot's head. Height: 6.8 inches. AFM. Center right: Human face surrounded by parrot heads with large crooked beaks. Diameter: 8.04 inches. AFM. Lower right: Handle in the shape of a badger (?) head, geometric line design. Diameter: 9.28 inches. AFM.

design elements on a gray or white background, or a red design on an orange-colored base. Around 700 A.D. creativity flowered in the form of pots shaped like birds, which are assumed to have been used to decorate graves—water carriers on the last journey. Black designs on a white background also became increasingly common. In specific areas one also finds black-on-red pottery as well as bowls that are a polished black on the inside and red or brownish on the outside.

At this stage, there appeared a clear difference between utilitarian pottery and that used for ceremonial purposes. The former, called "corrugated ware," had an exterior resembling corrugated iron. The spirals used to shape the pot were not scraped smooth; in fact, in the process of working the spirals by hand in order to seal the pot, the spirals were emphasized. The ceremonial pottery was characterized chiefly by painted designs, which became increasingly varied. The wares of Mesa Verde, Chaco Canyon and Kayenta are remarkable for the dynamic content of their compositions, made up of undulating and straight elements. Checkerboard patterns, zig-zag lines and parallels, triangles, rhomboids, herringbone patterns, concentric circles and other design elements came into play on the curved surfaces, taking possession of the rounded space and forming a harmonious whole in which extreme temperance is paired with great elegance. Symmetry and asymmetry alternated in an astonishingly fluid interchange that is surprisingly effective. Especially imaginative shapes were created between 1000 and 1100. Platters attached to one another are charac-teristic, as are the double mugs found at Mesa Verde and common there until 1300.

At this time Anasazi pottery making was at its peak: Bowls, platters, jars, water jars, mugs, ladles (these occur as half jars or as bowls with handles) and *kiva* jars (with a diameter of

Above and facing page: Four pieces of pottery from Casas Grandes (Mexico). From left to right: Pottery with an anthropomorphic shape, a caricatured face with prominent chin and cheeks that end in ears. The mouth is indicated. The whole piece is somewhat humorous, a not uncommon characteristic of southwestern pottery. Height: 6.24 inches. AFM. Anthropomorphic pot with extended legs, arms parallel to the body, shaped eyes and nose. Length: 9.32 inches. AFM. Red anthropomorphic pitcher with a flat head, almond-shaped eyes and shaped nose, chin and ears. Height: 7.6 inches. AFM. Double mug. A large number of these mugs were found at Mesa Verde. Diameter: 5 inches. AFM.

6 to 18 inches) competed with one another in beauty and elegance. Geometric patterns were artfully interwoven; the interaction of positive and negative contrasts was continually used in innovative ways.

The pottery of Chaco Canyon was characterized by hard, thin walls in an attractive white or gray, as well as rows of finely painted solid black triangles. Mesa Verde pottery was thick-walled and the rims tended to be square and flat. The background was pearly white with a hint of gray: A white slip covered the gray clay. Many pots were so highly polished that they seem translucent. The decoration consisted of spirals, stepped pyramids and band patterns. The design was generally more coarsely applied than in Chaco Canyon pottery. The corrugated ware was often decorated by scoring or notching the coils. It appears that by 1050 the iron content of clay was being used for black pigmentation, in addition to plant pigments, which produced a more sensual, velvety black. Kayenta pottery was sometimes so elaborately decorated with patterns in black—spirals, triangles within triangles, hatching and cross-hatching—that the white background all but disappeared. The pattern seems reversed, as though it were done in white on a black background.

Another variety of pottery that was common was polychrome, with black, red or white on an orange or yellow base. The Pueblos of the upper Rio Grande Valley in northern New Mexico made a black-on-yellow pottery and a polychrome variety was made between 1300 and 1600. In any event, the pottery of each region took on characteristic elements: Cylindrical pots were used in Chaco Canyon, jars in Mesa Verde, bowls with a single handle attached to the rim in Kayenta. These handles were often decorated with an animal sculpture, separately made and attached prior to firing.

Page 172: Mug, black on white, with characteristic Chaco Canyon (New Mexico) decoration consisting of geometric lines and crosshatching, handle in the shape of a jaguar (?). Height: 7.84 inches. HMP.

Page 173: Typical Chaco Canyon pottery, black on white, with stairway-like motifs, triangles, chessboard squares, elongated spirals and crosshatched areas. Anasazi Culture. Clockwise from upper left: Cylindrical pot. Height: 8.8 inches. MNM. Ladle in Mesa Verde style. Length: 13.6 inches. CCP. Ladle. Length: 5.2 inches. CCP. Bowl. Diameter: 8.0 inches. CCP. Bowl with painted rim. Diameter: 4.2 inches. CCP. Mug. Height: 6.8 inches. MMA.

Page 174: Animal designs on Mesa Verde pottery. From left to right: Schematized deer, stylized deer, stylized bird, perhaps a turkey. Mug House, Mesa Verde (Colorado), MVM.

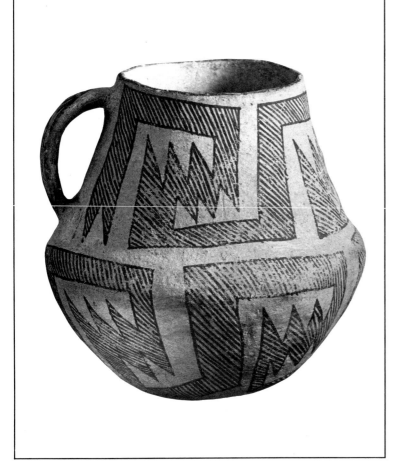

Like the Hohokam, the Anasazi of the Basketmaker III Period had an honored tradition in the art of making figurines. These female figures were crudely fashioned and generally not fired. Certain anatomical parts, such as the eyes, nose and breasts, were exaggerated and decorated with punctuations and scoring. A combination of realism and stylization gave them a remarkably expressive quality. Many decorated nipple-shaped objects have also been found; it has been suggested that they are connected with fertility rites.

The Fremont people also made clay and wood figurines that often represented couples, a man and a woman. Some had human bodies with the heads of birds, a motif also found in Hohokam society. Others represented animals and pregnant women. Many of these miniature sculptures were found in storage rooms, corroborating the theory that they were intended as guardian or fertility figurines.

There was an active exchange of pottery between peoples. Along with tons of sea shells from California, selenite (a variety of gypsum) pigments, iron pyrite crystals, copper and turquoise, wonderful objects from Casas Grandes, the main trade center with Meso-America (1060–1340), have been found at Mesa Verde. The Meso-American influence is clearly evident in its well-crafted pottery: vases in human, bird, animal and fish shapes, and colorful bowls and pots, painted in black and red on a base of golden brown or yellow, decorated with very complex geometric patterns.

Southwest pottery, although similar from region to region, is also clearly differentiated depending on its place of origin. The designs range from simple lines to complex naturalistic and geometric compositions, although it is not possible to explore these differences in detail here. The pottery produced by modern Pueblo people, especially that of the 19th and 20th

Right: Water jar (olla) in the shape of a bird, painted in reddish brown on white, with a stylized deer or antelope head; cult object (or mortuary offering). Height: 9.64 inches. Mogollon Culture, ASM.

Page 176: Olla with two handles, black motif on a yellowish base, decorated with suns, stars, curved lines and hatched areas. Height: 12.96 inches. Mesa Verde (Colorado), Anasazi Culture, UCM.

Page 177: Clockwise from upper left: Pitcher, black on white, richly painted, with handle in the shape of an animal (perhaps a dog with wings). Height: 7.32 inches. ASM. Mug, black on white. This drinking vessel was once broken and repaired in prehistoric times; the handle has a rare T-shaped cut-out. Height: 4 inches. Mesa Verde, Anasazi Culture, ASM. Corrugated ware with yucca fiber twine; the base is made of juniper bark. Height: 9.8 inches. Kayenta Region, Anasazi Culture, ASM. Water jar with incising. Length: 6.84 inches. Rio Grande Region, Anasazi Culture (Collection of A. Bandelier), ASM.

centuries, is often considered to be the pinnacle of the craft, although it represents only the absolutely logical conclusion of the pre-existing Anasazi tradition. This art, so highly developed in an environment so adverse to human life, was designed to fulfill very special needs, an excellent example of necessity influencing art forms. The formal beauty must be viewed within a framework of practical use. Take, for example, the most utilitarian pots of the Anasazi, the corrugated ware used for carrying water, cooking and storage. The rounded shape and ridged, parallel lines of the exterior represented the universe and the continuity of natural forces, while serving the practical purpose of making the vessel easy to handle. (Compared to pottery, the petroglyphs, discussed in the next chapter, can be seen as a virtual spiritual luxury.) Clara Lee Tanner, author of one of the most popular books about Southwest prehistoric crafts, writes: "Perhaps one of the reasons for such diversity in ceramics was because it was the chief vessel-producing craft" (*Southwestern Craft Art*, 1976).

Pottery making in the Southwest was a consummate art, realizing both the technical and the expressive potential of the medium. The plant and animal world, human beings and abstract spheres were all brought into play and synthesized with extraordinary mastery: Each part expressed the whole—*pars pro toto*. Each pot revealed an aspect of the universe, which was in turn suffused with the spirit of the natural forces. It is rare to find geometric abstract elements so completely harmonized with organic life as is the case with this art form, created out of the depth of the perception of the prehistoric Indians and their highly developed sense of harmony within their environment.

Left: Mesa Verde pottery: pots, pitchers and mugs, black on white with geometric designs. The double mug is among the most unusual pieces. Mesa Verde National Park (Colorado), MVM. Upper left: Water jar. Height: 3.0 inches. Wetherill Mesa (Colorado). Center: Double pitcher. Height: 3.8 inches. Lower left: *Kiva* pot. Height: 5.6 inches; diameter: 7.76 inches at the widest point. Long House. Right: Pitcher with handle. Height: 7.28 inches; diameter: 7 inches at widest point. Chapin Mesa.

Above: Three bowls found in Hopi graves that represent a link between prehistoric and historic times with their continuity in form and decorative motifs; UCM. From left to right: Bowl, brown on ochre, with schematized animal. Polychrome bowl with the magic hand symbol. Diameter: 10.56 inches. Polychrome bowl, arm and hand (with schematized fingernails). Diameter: 10.4 inches.

in incised petroglyphs at, for instance, the Galisteo site south of Santa Fe. They were decorated with bear paws and other motifs, probably clan symbols, which possessed magical powers to protect the owner.

It is difficult to date petroglyphs or even to attribute them to a particular culture. Since the Archaic Period, many different Indian peoples have lived in the Southwest, as roving hunters and gatherers or as sedentary farmers. Further, as of the 15th and 16th centuries the Apaches and Navajos have added their petroglyphs to those of the older cultures. Some of the pictographs may have been created during the second millennium before the birth of Christ and others may be as recent as the 12th century A.D., or even as late as the last century. Even contemporary Native Americans can provide little information about the creators or the significance of the pictures.

The dating of the various petroglyph sites is based on examination of a number of features: the patina on the stone, the several superimposed styles and techniques, the extent of the lichen growth and the degree of erosion that the stone has undergone. Nonetheless, given the current state of knowledge, dating is extremely approximate. (In one instance we can have some certainty: A picture of a horse has to postdate 1500, since horses were introduced to the Southwest by the Spaniards in the 16th century.) It has also been determined that many pictographs were "reworked" centuries later by other artists, which adds to the difficulty of determining age and origin.

Sometimes incised pictographs occur on small rocks placed at regular intervals around a house. Perhaps this was intended to mark the hunting and gathering territories of individual groups or clans. There are innumerable examples, although most are fairly recent, including representations of snakes, bear paws, lizards, bows, etc., all of which can be interpreted as clan symbols. Newspaper Rock in Indian Creek State Park in Utah and Willow Springs, near Tuba City, in northern Arizona are among the sites where the best examples of such motifs can be found. There are a total of 27 different symbols: hands, feet, ears of corn, sun circles, centipedes, bears, clouds, rabbits, coyotes and spiders among them.

What, then, is the meaning and purpose of the petroglyphs? This question can only be answered hypothetically, although the various theories extended are derived from the study of petroglyphs the world over. Some argue they represent magical acts, hunting rituals, historical events, caricatures, a pastime or a system of writing in hieroglyphics. In many cases the pictographs appear to be attempts to evoke those supernatural powers that affect the individual and collective welfare, such as the frequent occurrence of the lightning motif (as a zig-zag line), the cloud motif, snakes and other animals associated with water and thunderstorms, indispensable in such an arid environment. (In ancient Mexico the snake also represented the omnipotence of lightning.) They are frequently accompanied by erotic pictures of vulvae, phalluses and copulation. Certain hunting scenes may be interpreted as

Page 190: Large figures with shields decorated with animal symbols (bear paws). The surfaces and lines are fairly evenly picked. The style is a blend of realism, naturalistic stylization and schematization. Height of one figure: 46 inches. Galisteo (New Mexico).

Page 191: Rock engraving: human figures with feathers on their heads and decorated bodies, flanked by two stylized birds. The figure of Kokopelli, the hunchback flute player of the Southwest, can be seen to the right. The lower figure is 20 inches high and the upper one measures 24 inches. Galisteo (New Mexico).

Left: Petroglyphs that are clearly magical in character. The colored paints were made of mineral and plant materials and were probably applied to the rock with fingers. The figures pictured here were painted in red and ochre, the "shields" in black and white. Courthouse Wash, Arches National Park (Utah).

196

Page 194, Left: Detail of an enormous human figure. Large eyes scrutinize us; two animals (deer?) cover the upper body; Horseshoe Canyon, Canyonlands National Park (Utah).

Pages 194–195: Engraved and painted pictograph titled *The Three Kings*. The figures survey us with their dignified glance from a height of 100 feet. They were first picked and then emphasized with color; remnants of the original pigment (hematite) have survived. The schematic figure to the right is done in relief. Spirals and sun symbols are numerous. The figures are wearing feathers on their heads, necklaces around their necks and belts around their waists; the dots and lines on the torsos may represent tattoos or body paint. The highly ceremonial character of the entire composition is obvious. Dry Fork Canyon near Vernal (Utah).

the recapitulation of a successful hunt or the projection of one anticipated in the near future. Other scenes are surely of simple profane nature: references to daily activities, to religious rites and celebrations, to important annual events such as the summer and winter solstices. Klaus F. Wellmann, in his book *Muzzinabikon, Indianische Felsbilder Nordamerikas aus fünf Jahrtausenden* (1976), writes:

> The basis of all interpretations must be that an interpretation is possible only when all elements of the relevant cultural realm of the petroglyph being studied are considered. Many decades ago Franz Boas was able to prove that the same motif frequently means different things to different tribes. Theories which attempt a uniform interpretation of all Indian petroglyphs, as though they were equivalent to a written language or hieroglyphics (as Martineau was still doing in 1973), or to simply transfer the European categories, for example, without examining American circumstances lead to unreliable shortcuts and distortions of the hermeneutical abundance of North American petroglyphs.

In his book *The Rocks Begin to Speak* (1973), LeVan Martineau developed a theory that, although it has been questioned by others, provides an analysis of all etched and painted symbols from a simple curved line to human figures. Each of these pictographs has its own special meaning, he said, representing, for example, a spring, a cave, a path or a personality, while the detailed scenes report a real occurrence, like chronicles, pecked into the rock with scrupulous accuracy. According to this theory, all Southwest petroglyphs are a vast book "written" in hieroglyphics, wherein each sign represents a concept like "Caution, danger!" "Turn left," etc. The extremely abstract style in which many of the figures are painted, he argues, proves that they are not meant to be realistic representations, but to be precise geographical or historical statements.

It is hoped today that modern methods of study will provide a solid basis for the interpretation of abstract motifs in the complex petroglyphs of the Southwest. These methods include noting topographical features, the frequency of occurrence of individual images, their contemporaneity, location with respect to their figures, etc. The most recent research has shown that there is a uniformity in the pictorial and form language of the early Indian "artists" and their innumerable successors.

The pictures are not chaotic, although they may seem so at first glance, but are ordered in ways not previously understood. It has, for instance, been determined that the famous cave paintings of Lascaux are carefully ordered as to the succession and repetition of images; the placement of figures was not a matter of chance. The complexity and blending of meanings have also been noted: The petroglyphs are not just religious or metaphysical, but also profane. The mundane is always present in the transcendental. In this respect Indian pictographs are typical of those found around the world: If scenes of magical significance (like hunting) occur frequently in a given picture, then there will also be several scenes of practical daily life.

Left: A cat-like beast of prey (a mountain lion?) engraved on a sandstone block. The animal is stylized; the vertical, stiff legs are juxtaposed with the curved line of the torso, which is repeated in the tail. The artist intended a certain realism: He emphasized the curved claws and gave the animal two large eyes and a wide open mouth. Length: 30 inches. Rainbow Forest Museum, Petrified Forest National Park (Arizona).

Page 198: Petroglyphs, a magical scene with stylized figures. The largest has a body in the shape of a trapezoid. The lines are pecked; straight and curved lines harmonize with each other. The artist sought to balance the smooth surfaces with those that are pecked out. The representation is clear. Earrings, necklaces and feathers are the prevailing ornamentation; there is a magnificently decorated shield (12.8 inches diameter), which is carried by two people. McKee Springs, Dinosaur National Monument (Utah).

The discovery of a large amount of pottery spanning several centuries has proven to be a considerable help to researchers studying Southwest petroglyphs, since the same symbols and design elements are found on both. With their petroglyphs, the prehistoric Pueblo cultures have left us a visible record of their thoughts and the contours of their world (while oral histories and traditions change over time). The prehistoric peoples of the Southwest, the Mogollon, Hohokam and Anasazi, possessed a culture as varied and rich as that of 20th-century man.

Page 199: Petroglyphs, very geometrically shaped figures with trapezoidal bodies, a decorated shield, feather headdresses and necklaces. Several lines were made by fine and consistent pecking, others were incised with the edge of a stone ax. The height of the human figure at the bottom right is 40 inches. Dry Fork Canyon, Uintah Basin Area (Utah).

Above: Ten faces from a frieze called *The Thirteen Faces*. Polychrome painting of heads, which have masks and feather headdresses. Horse Canyon, Canyonlands National Park (Utah).

Right: Upper panel: Painted, mysterious shapes. The diameter of the concentric circle on the left is 74.4 inches. Near Salt Creek Canyon, Canyonlands National Park (Utah). Below: Paintings of "warriors" with richly embellished shields behind which only the heads and feet are visible; above them a frieze of dots. Figure to the left is 17.6 inches high. Peek-Aboo Spring, Salt Creek Canyon.

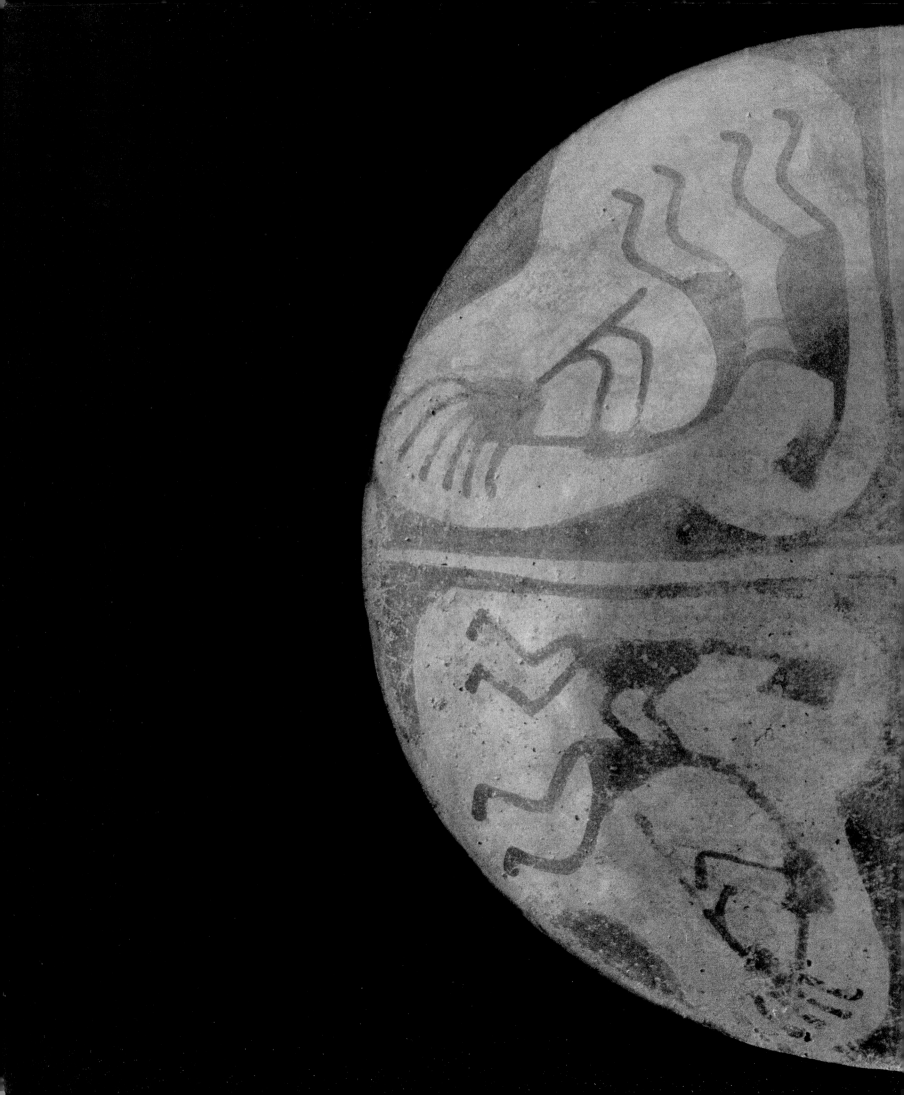

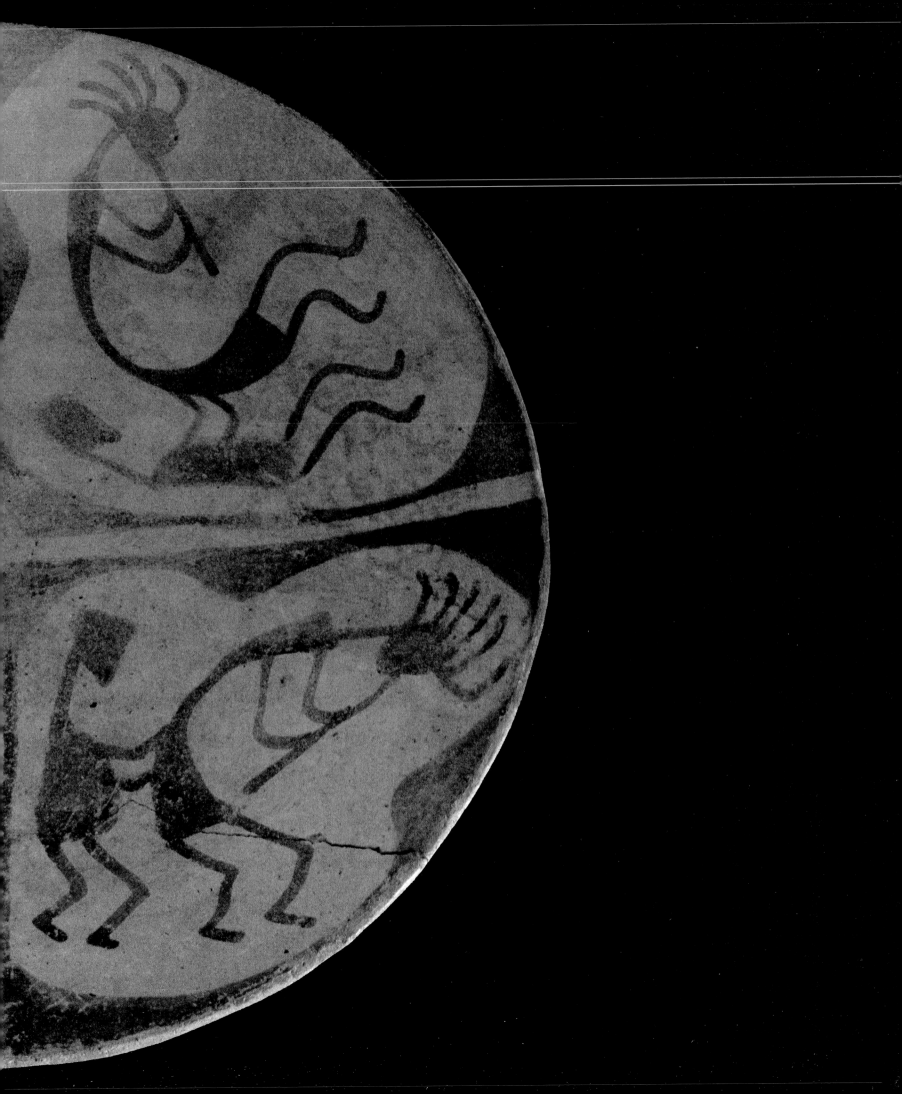

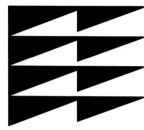

MOTIFS AND SYMBOLS

The first scientific study of American petroglyphs and their symbolic content, published in 1893, was *Picture Writing of the American Indians*, by Garrick Mallery. One-quarter of this 800-page work, which is still used as a source book, is dedicated to southwestern pictographs. Mallery was also one of the first to establish the many close similarities of Indian cultures to cultures on other continents and illustrate the universality of the vocabulary of the prehistoric Indian petroglyphs in the Four Corners Area.

We will, of course, never comprehend the precise meaning of many of the signs—only their creators could explain them! Even now, more than 60 percent of the abstract elements of southwestern pictographs cannot be interpreted clearly. Several of these symbols, however, have appeared at different times all over the world. If they are used in clearly defined pictographs, it is more likely that their meaning may be discovered. Since the archetypes have lived within us since our beginnings, as Carl Jung's studies have argued, it is possible to gain insights into the meaning of the southwestern petroglyphs through comparisons with petroglyphs of other cultures. The strong formal and spiritual inner relationship of pictographic art worldwide is one of the mysteries that holds great fascination for us: Its harmony is analogous to the inorganic and organic coherence of our universe, which is mysterious and logical at the same time, insofar as all of it springs from the same elemental particles of matter.

Petroglyphs were probably also a sort of chronicle for prehistoric Indian people in which concepts, legends and contemporaneous events were "written down." The innumerable engravings found in Arizona provide the Hopi, for instance, with information about the migrations of the clans; sometimes rows of vertical lines are represented in combination with animals and it seems reasonable to assume that this is "information" about the numbers and types of animals brought along. It is in any event certain that many symbols, such as coyote heads, clouds (three semicircles that culminate in vertical lines representing rain) or the humpbacked flute player Kokopelli, were clan symbols. This may well be the case for other abstract symbols that have not yet been interpreted. Perhaps certain rock walls covered with apparently randomly placed figures are in fact organized according to strict rules, a carefully defined ritual, designed to serve as reminders of the details of songs, prayers and dances during the long, holy ceremonies.

Pages 202–203: Shallow bowl, red on ochre. The composition is made up of four symmetrical sections of a circle, each depicting a dancer holding the waist of Kokopelli, the hunchback flute player, shown wearing a feather headdress. The bent legs and body indicate the movement of the dance. Diameter: 10.84 inches. Snaketown (Arizona), Hohokam Culture, ASM.

Right: A variety of signs and symbols—spirals, a snake, the sun, corn stalks, a labyrinth, very schematic human figures etc.—are clearly visible against the black and brown patina of the sandstone. Inscription Point, near Wupatki National Monument (Arizona).

Page 206: Geometric designs are called labyrinths, a common motif found on Southwest pottery and baskets, but also in other parts of the world, such as Crete or the Italian Val Camonica. Length: approximately 48 inches. Magnetic Masa, Wupatki National Monument (Arizona).

Many *kivas* were decorated with frescoes, either individual paintings or richly illustrated, polished compositions. Examples range from white big-horned sheep on a red background, found on a house post over a geometrical pattern, in a complex combination in which red and white achieve a remarkable amount of perspective, to the beautiful paintings in the *kivas* of Pueblo Kuaua (in Coronado State Monument, New Mexico), a magnificent summation of the earlier Anasazi creations, most of which have not survived.

In the painted *kiva* of Kuaua, a village built on the Rio Grande around 1300, 17 layers of multicolored frescoes on 68 plaster surfaces were discovered, around 400 representations of difficult-to-interpret motifs originating in the 15th century. They are apparently fertility symbols, ritual hunting scenes, rain ceremonies, clan symbols, illustrations of creation myths, etc. The upper layers have been removed and preserved and can now be viewed in the small museum next to the Visitor Center. More noteworthy are the many frescoes of Awatovi and Kawaika-a in the Jeddito Valley and those of Pottery Mound in the Rio Puerco Valley, where there are more than 100 layers of paintings one on top of the other.

Circles and stars, undoubtedly sun symbols, are extremely numerous. Representations of the planets and stars, including paintings that reflect precise observations of comets and shooting stars, were discovered in northern Arizona. One of the best known astronomical pictures is a painting done in ochre and red named *Supernova*, which was found in Chaco Canyon in New Mexico. It consists of a star with 10 points, a quarter moon and a magical "positive" hand. It has been theorized that it depicts the explosion of a supernova transformed into a sacred picture. (Japanese and Chinese chronicles also note this astronomical event, following which the giant star was visible in the sky for 23 days in July of the year 1054.) The supernova is painted next to a waxing moon that, according to calculations made by contemporary astronomers, must have been located near the giant star in the precise position in which it is shown in the petroglyph. Two other virtually identical representations of this event have been found in Arizona.

One of the most common symbols in southwestern art was the hand, universal symbol of protection against evil spirits and a sort of individual signature. In Galisteo, south of Santa Fe, an entire stone wall is covered with hands in all sizes, dynamically distributed. Hands are often the sole motif of large friezes, as in the Cave of the Twenty Hands in Canyonlands National Park or under Kachina Bridge in Natural Bridges National Monument, both in Utah. The hands were made the same way here as they were in Europe at the La Madeleine Cliff and in Australia: by laying the hand, fingers spread, against the rock and blowing paint around it through a hollow bone or a wooden tube (resulting in the pattern of a "negative" hand), or by pressing the paint-covered hand against the rock (a positive hand). (Footprints are also common in the Southwest.) The imprinting of the hand was undoubtedly a magical act, a visual sign of the wish that that which was pictured next to the hand could be attained:

Page 207: A selection of patterns from southeastern petroglyphs, created between 900 and 1300 A.D. at Three Rivers Petroglyph Site (New Mexico) and one from Nine Mile Canyon (Utah). Clockwise from upper left: Foot and geometric design with axial symmetry. Height: 8 inches. Sun symbol. Diameter: 6.8 inches. Geometric design with axial symmetry. 17.6 inches a side. Five concentric circles, interconnected with lines, perhaps sun symbols. Nine Mile Canyon. Stairway to heaven or stepped pyramid. Height: 14.8 inches. Concentric circles. Diameter: 15.6 inches.

Left: Pottery in the Ramos polychrome style: effigy of a seated woman nursing a child; decorated with black and red designs of universal symbolic significance: the "stairway to heaven" and clouds, the chessboard, the spiral (symbol of fertility) and the lightning sign, which heralds rain (on the left leg). Height: 8.04 inches. Casas Grandes (Mexico), ASM.

clouds for rain, for example, an ear of corn for a good harvest, or a big-horned sheep for a successful hunt. Series of hands are likely to have lent the site a highly sacred and spiritual character.

Another common symbol was the snake, a more or less undulating line, feathered, horned or rolled into spirals (similar in form to Quetzalcoatl, the "Feathered Serpent" and chief god in the cultures of the high valleys of Mexico). Representations of snakes, sometimes rudimentary, sometimes stylized or pictured in complex detail, are in evidence all over the Southwest, on frescoes in *kivas*, on pottery and in pictographs. Particularly beautiful examples, decorated with feathers and horns, their tails ending in three points, have been found in the Galisteo Basin. Perhaps, as was the case in Meso-America, they were the guardian spirits of springs and rivers. Feathers generally represent the Great Spirit, the father of all things. The myth of the Meso-American "cosmic snake" is associated with the corn cult: the ideal harmony of heaven and earth. In New Mexico the feathered or cloud snake is pictured as a reptilian body carrying a cumulus cloud on its back; its tongue is the jagged lightning.

Birds are common motifs found on both pottery and in petroglyphs. Representations of human beings with bird heads are very numerous, especially in Canyon de Chelly. Similar pictures have been found in Lascaux and Pech-Merle in France. Clay figurines of bird women have been found in excavations in the Mesapotamian Ur, although the best known examples are the ancient Egyptian frescoes of the god Horus with a hawk's head. The Zuni and Hopi believe the bird to be the receptacle of the soul and many cultures believe that the soul, after the death of the body, is carried away by a bird on a "magical flight." Many Indian people believe that the bird figures at Canyon de Chelly represent shamans, to whom the mystery of these magical soul flights was known. The bird is also frequently found at the top of a stepped pyramid, symbol of the ascent. To the Hopi, the bird also has the supernatural ability to communicate with the gods.

The figure of the humpbacked flute player Kokopelli is found throughout the Four Corners Area down through northern Mexico; innumerable images of him are seen on pots and in petroglyphs. His image has even been found in Canada and in South America. His was perhaps one of the most beloved images, first appearing with the Basketmakers around 700. He is a central figure in Hohokam and Mimbres pottery, a sort of leitmotiv. He is variously represented: The classical image of him is a crooked stick figure blowing into what appears to be a pipe. The humped back may or may not be emphasized, and is sometimes absent. Occasionally he carries a bow and arrows or has an enormous phallus. Some interpret him to be a fertility symbol and connect him with the harvest; for others he represents a sort of medicine man who wanders from tribe to tribe mediating quarrels and trading. In the latter role he does not have a humped back but carries a basket and represents the principle that unifies the various southwestern cultures, an American Mercury, god of

Left: The spiral and swastika are universal signs. They are found in the megalithic architecture on Malta, on African pottery, in Carnac, in the heart of the Sahara, and in the petroglyphs and pottery of the Southwest, such as that of the Anasazi pot at the far left. Black on white, 17.2 inches high, MNA. Below left: A shallow bowl in the shape of a turtle shell. Length: 6.16 inches. Casas Grandes (Mexico), AFM.

Above top: Spiral swastika from a Hohokam mortuary offering, Pueblo Grande Museum, Phoenix (Arizona). Below: Fremont petroglyph, a schematic person with a spiraled chest. Fremont River Gorge, Capitol Reef National Park (Utah). Left: The wavy line ending in a spiral represents a snake, symbol of fertility (drawing based on a photograph). The original engraving is located in Nine Mile Canyon (Utah).

commerce and good relations. Among contemporary Hopi, Kokopelli is the symbol of the flute clan. He is the go-between between men and the gods and carries grain and plant seeds in his "humped back." By playing his flute he creates the warmth necessary to germinate the seeds and allows friendship and harmony to flourish. Among the Zuni he is the "rain priest."

In other world cultures, the flute also represents rain and lightning and is therefore a fertility symbol. The flute player of the Andes is well known. As late as the last century he wandered from village to village with his flute and grain sack. There are also the marble sculptures (2600–2000 B.C.) of the flute player who accompanied the dead at Kykladen. Another example is the youth in an Etruscan fresco from the Grave of the Leopards in Tarquinia (fifth century B.C.), who plays two flutes. There is a representation of Kokopelli with two flutes in Walnut Canyon, and in Monticello, Utah, he leads a dance in which a row of triangular figures hold hands. Certainly Kokopelli is to the Southwest what Pan or Orpheus represented in Greek culture, a multilayered "hero," go-between between heaven and earth, the connecting link between various worlds, master of ceremonies.

Another symbol seen in southwestern art is the labyrinth found in the Galisteo Basin area of Arizona and New Mexico. Identical images have been found on Crete, in Ireland, on the Etruscan coast and in the Italian Val Camonica. Depicted as a spiraling line, the labyrinth represents the myth of mankind to the Hopi people. It gives visible form to the road man must travel as he emerges from mother earth and follows the path of his life.

Other puzzling motifs no doubt represent archetypal elements, such as the "heart line," which runs from the mouth of an animal to its organs, ending in an arrowhead. This motif, which may portend a successful hunt, is found in Virginia, Utah and New Mexico as well as in La Madeleine, France, Norway and Siberia, and is still used in Zuni art today. Dots

Above: On pottery as well as in pictographs universal signs are found over and over: zig-zag lines (representing lightning), tadpole or frog (water), the triangle, dot, etc. From left to right: Mimbres bowl, black on white. Diameter: 14.24 inches. HMP. Mimbres bowl, black on white, stylized insects and parallel lines. Diameter: 18.28 inches. UCM. Shallow bowl, black on gray. Diameter: about 14.4 inches. Jemez Pueblo (New Mexico), 1300-1600, MNM.

Right: Several representations of Kokopelli, the hunchback flute player. Top: Double image, reminiscent of the flute player of the Andes or of Greece. Height: 14.4 inches. Walnut Canyon National Monument (Arizona). Below, from left to right: Petroglyphs in Horseshoe Canyon, Canyonlands National Park (Utah). Incising, 16.8 inches high. Tsankawi, Bandelier National Monument (New Mexico). A pottery shard with the image of Kokopelli, Mesa Verde (Colorado), MVM.

The spiral is a fertility symbol the world over, found, for example, in the megalith art of Malta and Carnac in Brittany, in Cretan art, as well as among the petroglyphs of the Sahara and the Vallée des Merveilles at Monte Bego on the French-Italian border. Double spirals frequently decorate the rims of corrugated ware found at Mesa Verde. The image that comes to mind is of a steady flow of ceramic waves, symbol of constancy, and embedded within it, everlasting fertility. Spirals are heavily represented throughout the Southwest. Pecked or painted onto stone, they are found within complex structured pictographs, but also isolated or grouped with other geometric patterns, such as the sun, the moon and other elements. There are naturally occurring spirals in the animal and plant world (snails, grape vines) that transmit a feeling of eternity, with symbolic affinities with the moon and the womb. Even today the Zuni, at the ceremony celebrating the winter solstice, sing "spiral songs" and dance "spiral dances," which are reminiscent of the Muslim whirling dervishes.

It seems certain that many of the geometric patterns of the petroglyphs originated in the ornamentation of baskets and pottery. One of the most common is the stepped pyramid, the "stairway to heaven." "To the Indians," said A. Bandelier, "the clouds are the stairs which lead to heaven." The stepped pyramid represents the ascent of man into higher worlds. The pattern is found on *kiva* walls, on the walls of houses (inverted at Long House, Bandelier) and on stone walls under rock shelters. In ancient Egyptian texts the stairs were also one of the many ways by means of which the dead pharaoh could attain entrance into the heavens: The pyramid, a double staircase connecting heaven and earth, symbolized this ascent. It is amazing—or maybe not—that the same motif is found several millennia later in petroglyphs thousands of miles from the Valley of the Kings.

Finally, in view of the many turquoise fragments found in the bundles of medicine men it can be assumed that the color also had a very special significance. In ancient Egypt green symbolized fertility, while blue represented truth. In Meso-American cultures turquoise represented fire and the sun. The Navajo sun god rode on a turquoise horse in his heavenly orbit.

Above: Engraving of stylized birds. The bird is among the most important symbols of the Southwest, as well as of the American continent as a whole: It embodies the eternal and has the task of carrying the soul of the dead into the beyond.

Right: The stepped pyramid, or "stairway to heaven," symbolizes rain clouds as well as the paths that lead into the next world (as in ancient Egypt). The design is commonly found on pottery and in pictographs. Top: Painting of a frieze of birds sitting on the top of three pyramids, red on ochre. Height: 7.2 inches. Gila Cliff Dwellings National Monument (New Mexico). Lower left: Painting inside a room at Long House Ruin. Length: 50.4 inches. Bandelier National Monument (New Mexico). Lower right: The church at the present Taos Pueblo (New Mexico), where the architecture appears, in its own fashion, to perpetuate the power of the universal symbol.

The Pueblo Indians were a cheap, readily available source of labor for the ranches, mines and building projects. Outraged by the persecution and exploitation to which they were subjected, the Indians organized a revolt in 1680 and drove out the Spaniards, who returned 12 years later with a larger army and succeeded in putting down further revolts until 1736. Nevertheless, the rebellions brought about improved conditions and political and religious pressures decreased. Because of their geographic distance from the areas settled by the Spanish colonists, only the Hopi were able to remain relatively independent.

In 1821 Mexico gained independence from Spain and governed New Mexico for the next 25 years. During this period, the Navajo and other nomadic tribes, such as the Utes and Comanches, took advantage of Mexico's neglect of the area to intensify their raids on Pueblo villages. War between Mexico and the United States broke out in 1846 and the Treaty of Guadalupe Hidalgo in 1848, which ended the war, declared most of New Mexico, Arizona and California to be U.S. territory. The new government provided for law and order and put an end to the Navajo raids.

As Protestantism established itself in the Southwest beginning about 1850, the power of the Catholic Church diminished. This meant greater freedom for Pueblo people, who could once again practice their own religion. It would be nearly a century before the Indians were granted full voting rights as citizens in 1924 and later legislation gave them the full possession of their reservations.

Since the 1950s a revitalization of Pueblo culture has been underway: The population has increased, medical and hygienic conditions have improved, native religious practices have been revived and the Pueblo people have become more aware of their legal rights. Their crafts (pottery, jewelry, blanket making and basketry) developed rapidly and many artists have become known even outside the Southwest (Maria Martinez, for instance, from Pueblo Ildefonso, became famous for her magnificent black and polychrome pottery before her death in 1980). Nonetheless, in many communities living conditions could be much improved.

Many Pueblo people remain true to their Indian identity and larger numbers are becoming actively involved in the traditions of their ancestors. Although certain ceremonies are staged for the tourist trade, they nonetheless help to revitalize the ancient ways. In many villages the ceremonies are performed in secret, Taos and Santo Domingo being among the least accessible to outsiders. Many of the Pueblo communities may be visited if permission is first granted and a payment made. A calendar of ceremonies open to the public can be obtained in all larger New Mexico communities or at tribal offices.

Although the Pueblo cultures, in contrast to those of other Indian peoples, appear to the outsider to be virtually identical to one another, this is not the case. Language, customs and religious practices can vary fundamentally from village to village: A Pueblo Indian from south of Santa Fe will be unlikely to understand a Pueblo from north of Santa Fe.

The Pueblo Indians, the West and the 20th Century

Since the beginning of this century the lifestyle and art of the Pueblo Indians, the descendants of the most significant prehistoric Indian culture of the American Southwest, have increasingly influenced Western society, especially its artists and writers. Many artists have lived with the Zuni and Hopi and have given realistic or poetic expression to their impressions and influences.

Among these visitors was the great Swiss psychologist Carl Gustav Jung, who frequently mentions the Pueblo people in his work *Psychology and Alchemy*. In a study of the symbolism of the mandala and other universal shapes, he makes connections between these shapes and the world view of the Hopi and Anasazi. In his autobiography, *Memories, Dreams, Reflections*, he quotes an Indian man named Mountain Lake who, during a conversation, explained the following about the Pueblo religion: "We are a people who live on the top of the world, we are the sons of our father the sun, and with our religion we help our father every day to make his journey across the sky. We do this not only for ourselves, but for the whole world. If we can no longer practice our religion then within ten years the sun will no longer rise. Then it will always be night."

The English novelist D.H. Lawrence lived near Taos for a long time. He also visited the reservations of the Apaches, Navajos and Hopis. He was fascinated by their rituals and ceremonies. "Mornings in Mexico" describes a Hopi corn and snake dance. About the Anasazi ruins he remarked: "Why they have not fallen into dust is a mystery. That these rectangular piles of clay have survived the centuries, while the Greek marble sculptures crumble and the cathedrals sway, herein lies the miracle. But the bare human hand with a little fresh, soft mud is quicker than time and defies the centuries."

The well-known French anthropologist Claude Levi-Strauss also studied Pueblo culture, concentrating especially on the parallels between Pueblo society and other cultures on the American continent, especially the myths of the Mimbreno Apaches. He wrote the foreword to the French edition of *Sun Chief*, the autobiography of the Hopi Don C. Talayesva. The French writer André Malraux owned a collection of kachina dolls. These dolls and the multicolored sand paintings of the Navajo, which keep the origin myths alive, and the designs found on Indian pottery, have also inspired surrealistic artists of Europe.

In his writings, André Breton, the high priest of surrealism, frequently discussed the meaning of the creative impulse as it manifests itself in the Indian societies of the Southwest and how, although confined within a precise, formal style, it escapes its boundaries time and time again and devolves into free forms in celebration of nature and life. He praised Indian art for challenging the antithesis between sculptural forms and decorative two-dimensionality, particularly in pottery, expressing the metaphors of the spiritual as well as the natural world. He found in this a model for the suggestive images of his poetry. In 1945

Above: Hopi pot, black on ochre, cylindrical shape, with stylized bird design, made about 1930. Height: 9.6 inches. MVM.

he traveled in Arizona and New Mexico, and was so impressed by what he saw that he designated it the center of the world, the home of the creator of universal harmony. He wrote: "I greet you at the foot of the ladder, which disappears into the mystery of the Hopi Kiva, that underground, sacred chamber, on this 22nd day of August 1945, in Mishongnovi, at the hour when snakes in one last revolution declare their preparedness to complete the union with the human mouth."

The German artist Max Ernst was also fascinated by the Southwest. His two famous paintings entitled *Petrified City* appear to anticipate this interest: They remind us of the Pueblo ruins high up on the mesas. Ernst lived in Sedona, Arizona with his American wife, the painter Dorothea Tanning, and accumulated a significant kachina collection, which, beginning in 1944, inspired his sculptures. Like Pueblo art, his works are symbolic rather than realistic or purely abstract. His painting *Moon Over Sedona* gives marvelous expression to the unique Southwest atmosphere of aridity and spirituality. Before Ernst, the great German expressionist Emil Nolde was influenced by kachina art.

The French surrealist Yves Tanguy was also inspired by the Southwest, which he visited in the 1940s. Many reflections of this experience are found in his landscapes, where he regularly rediscovered the enormous mesas and needle-shaped upthrusting rock formations of Arizona and New Mexico.

Recent and contemporary American art more and more draws on the rich vocabulary of prehistoric Indian people, sometimes unconsciously, in other instances in response to immediate influences. The abstraction of sign and symbol is combined with anthropomorphic and zoomorphic representations and thereby connected to an archetypal vision of the universal. These artists place emphasis on the shamanistic aspect, the desire for unity with nature, a new, "more primitive" perception. To mention only a few artists who were enthusiastic about the Southwest: Georgia O'Keefe, Adolph Gottlieb, who frequently used an appropriate characterization of Pueblo art: "We prefer the simple expression of complex thoughts"; and Frank Stella, in his *Indian Bird Series* from the 1970s. Jackson Pollock studied Garrick Mallery's important book *Picture Writing of the American Indians*, and declared: "I have always been impressed by the plastic quality of Indian art. The Indians are true artists, both through their ability to find the appropriate image and through their ability to comprehend the object, the subject matter of their art."

The influence can also be found in Michael Heizer's monumental sculptures, like *Frog Effigy*, the frog having symbolized water to the Hohokam; Charles Simonds, whose miniature clay sculptures are reminiscent of cliff houses and *kivas*; James Havard, with his painting of Zuni masks; and finally, Jasper Johns, one of the greatest artists of the late 20th century. It is not an accident that he rediscovered the symbolism of the ancient Pueblo Indians in his works and used the colors red, yellow and blue, which have traditional significance.

Above: A Hopi silversmith at work. The Hopi and Zuni are considered masters in the creation of silver jewelry set with turquoise and other semiprecious stones.

Right, above: Taos Pueblo, north of Santa Fe, New Mexico, with its terraced houses and ladders and bread ovens in the forefront. Lower left: Walpi, a contemporary Hopi pueblo. One has to imagine the Anasazi pueblos on the Colorado Plateau centuries ago, situated this way and appearing exactly like this one. First Mesa (Arizona). Lower right: Navajo Indian woman weaving a blanket. Since the introduction of sheep into the Southwest by the Spanish, the Navajo have been known for their magnificent, colorful wool blankets with their rich and artistic geometric patterns.

In the fundamental work *Primitivism in Twentieth-Century Art,* edited by William Rubin, historic and prehistoric Pueblo culture is mentioned. References are made to the relationship between Zuni art and the works of Paul Klee; the Hopi kachinas and Emil Nolde; American Indian symbols and Marsden Hartley, in whose eyes the Indian is "one of the important decorators of the planet"; Zuni art and Man Ray ("Totem"); and so on.

Now, as in the past, great works of art trace the shortest path from one culture to another, and the magnificent artistic creations of the Pueblos seem to us both mysteriously ancient and strikingly modern.

Opposite right: Hopi kachina doll from about 1901. The kachinas are the supernatural beings personified by masked dancers in the important religious ceremonies. This colorfully painted doll carved of poplar wood is richly decorated and carries a bow. Height: approximately 12 inches. HMP. Below: A work by the contemporary Swiss artist Urs Huber, who lived in the Southwest and returns to it often to be inspired by the myths of contemporary Pueblo people. Title: *Meeting,* 23.2 x 27.2 inches, various techniques, 1986.

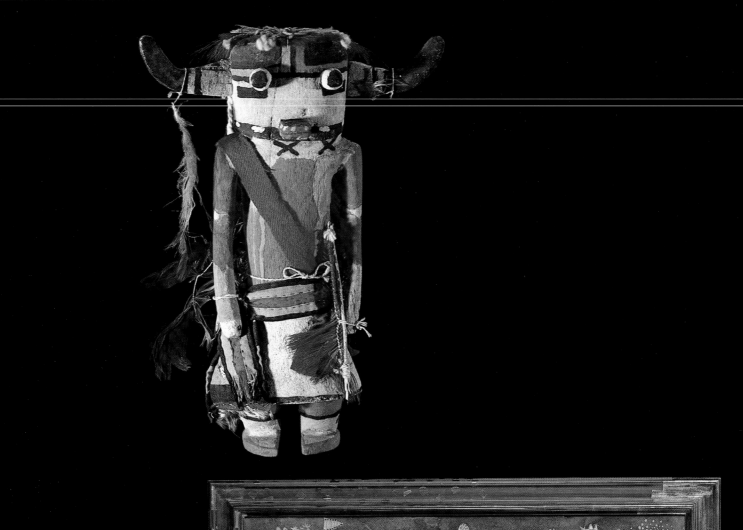

OVERVIEW OF THE SOUTHWEST

All parks, museums and places of interest are presented alphabetically by state (Arizona, Colorado, New Mexico and Utah). Informative brochures and other pertinent literature are available at the museums, national parks and national monuments; many sites have gift shops offering quality Indian crafts. As to the locations of petroglyphs, it is recommended that one inquire at the visitor center about guided tours or necessary permission; some areas are not easily accessible or require a permit.

ARIZONA

Canyon de Chelly National Monument

Visitor center, museum, petroglyphs. Anasazi Culture. Access is difficult. Three of the most spectacular canyons of the Southwest are part of this federally protected area: *Canyon de Chelly, Canyon del Muerto* and *Monument Canyon*. There are approximately 140 village sites here. Continually inhabited from the fourth to the 14th century, all types of Anasazi architecture are represented in this area, from simple pit houses to multi-story pueblos. The famous *Mummy Cave* with its two-story tower is located in Canyon del Muerto. Other well-known sites are *Antelope House* and *White House*, the upper section of which is whitewashed. It was inhabited from the 11th to the 13th century and had a population of about 100 people. With its 175 rooms and four *kivas*, all built of masonry, White House is comparable to the Mesa Verde and Aztec pueblos.

Casa Grande Ruins National Monument

Visitor center, museum. Hohokam Culture. The *Great House*, a massive three-story building surrounded by a square wall (415×227 feet) dominates the complex of ruins, which stretches over 1.5 square miles. Casa Grande was inhabited from 1350 until 1450. It was constructed of large calishe blocks, a limestone composite rock, and the foundation measures 60×40 feet. An unattractive metal support, built in 1932, holds up the main structure. Was the large house a ceremonial building, an observatory, home of a leader, or a community center? The early excavators found pottery, sleeping mats, corn cobs, textile fragments, and other artifacts common to all the pueblos. Casa Grande and, 24 miles to the north, Snaketown, the Hohokam "capital" (not open to visitors), are the richest sites in southern Arizona (the future name for both sites is Hohokam-Pima National Monument).

Chiricahua National Monument

Visitor center. Marvelous landscape with fantastic rock formations created millions of years ago by volcanic activity.

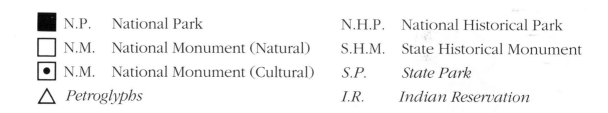

■	N.P.	National Park	N.H.P.	National Historical Park
□	N.M.	National Monument (Natural)	S.H.M.	State Historical Monument
⊡	N.M.	National Monument (Cultural)	*S.P.*	*State Park*
△	*Petroglyphs*		*I.R.*	*Indian Reservation*

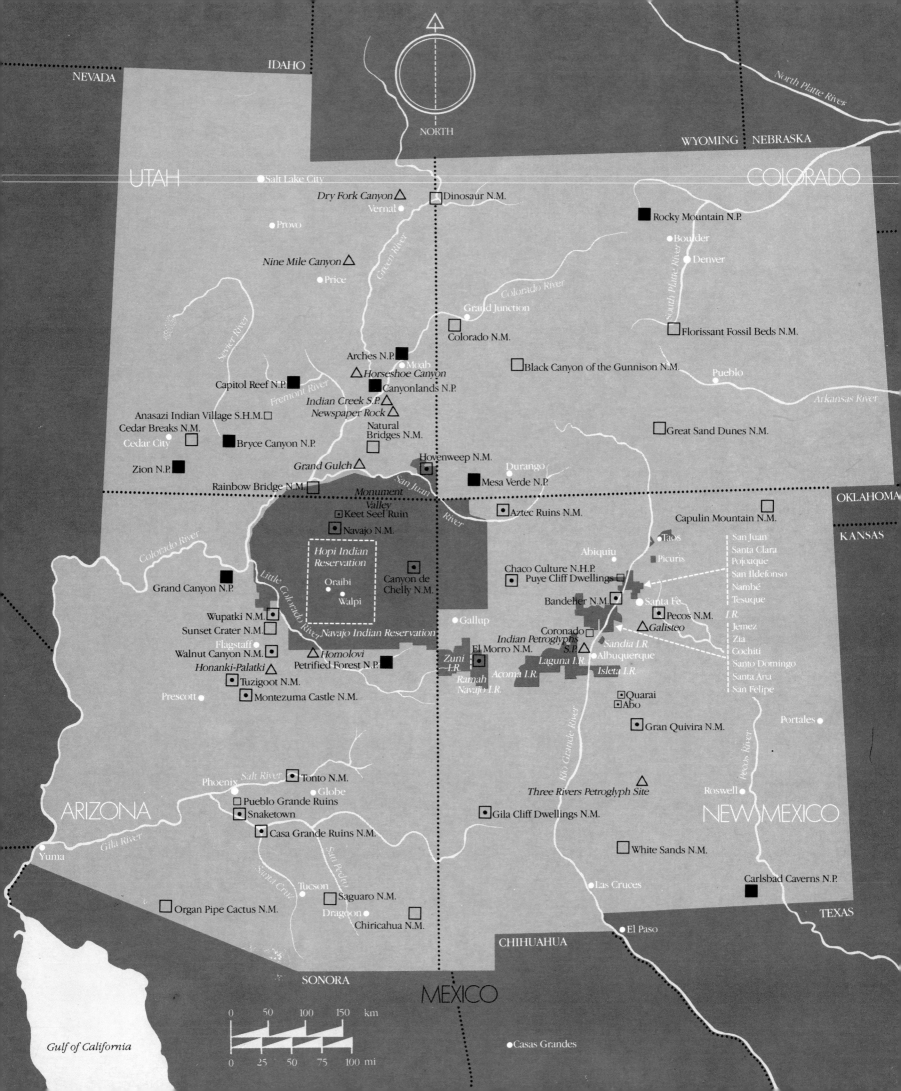

NORTH

NEVADA
IDAHO

WYOMING   NEBRASKA

UTAH   COLORADO

●Salt Lake City

Dry Fork Canyon △   □ Dinosaur N.M.
Vernal ●

Rocky Mountain N.P. ■

●Provo
●Boulder

Nine Mile Canyon △
●Denver

●Price

Green River

Colorado River

South Platte River

●Grand Junction

Florissant Fossil Beds N.M. □

Arches N.P. ■
□ Colorado N.M.

●Moab
Black Canyon of the Gunnison N.M. □

Capitol Reef N.P. ■   △ *Horseshoe Canyon*
●Pueblo

■ Canyonlands N.P.
Arkansas River

Fremont River   *Indian Creek S.P.* △

Anasazi Indian Village S.H.M. □   *Newspaper Rock* △
Cedar Breaks N.M.   □ Great Sand Dunes N.M.

Cedar City ●   Natural
■ Bryce Canyon N.P.   Bridges N.M.
□

Zion N.P. ■   *Grand Gulch* △   Hovenweep N.M.
●Durango

Rainbow Bridge N.M. □   San Juan   ■ Mesa Verde N.P.

Monument   River   OKLAHOMA

Valley   ● Aztec Ruins N.M.
● *Keet Seel Ruin*   Capulin Mountain N.M. □

⊙ Navajo N.M.
KANSAS

Colorado River   Hopi Indian
Reservation   ●Taos
San Juan

Abiquiu ●   Santa Clara
●Picuris   Pojoaque

Oraibi ●   Chaco Culture N.H.P.   San Ildefonso
Little Colorado River   Canyon de   ⊙ Puye Cliff Dwellings □   Nambé
Walpi ●   Chelly N.M.   Tesuque

Grand Canyon N.P. ■   Bandelier N.M. □   ● Santa Fe   *I.R.*

Wupatki N.M. ⊙   ● Gallup   Pecos N.M. □   Jemez
Zia
Sunset Crater N.M. □   △ *Galisteo*   Cochiti
Flagstaff ●   Coronado □   Santo Domingo
Walnut Canyon N.M. ⊙   *Indian Petroglyphs*   Santa Ana
Homolovi △   *S.P.* △ *Sandia I.R.*   San Felipe
Honanki-Palatki △   El Morro N.M. □   ● Albuquerque
⊙ Tuzigoot N.M.   *Zuni*   *Laguna I.R.*
⊙ Montezuma Castle N.M.   *I.R.*   *Acoma I.R.*   *Isleta I.R.*
Prescott ●   Petrified Forest N.P. ■

Ramah   ⊙ Quarai
Navajo I.R.   ⊙ Abo
●Portales

⊙ Gran Quivira N.M.

Salt River   ⊙ Tonto N.M.

Phoenix ●   Roswell ●
Globe ●   Three Rivers Petroglyph Site △

□ Pueblo Grande Ruins   NEW MEXICO
⊙ Snaketown   ⊙ Gila Cliff Dwellings N.M.

⊙ Casa Grande Ruins N.M.

ARIZONA   □ White Sands N.M.

Gila River

●Yuma   Santa Cruz   ●Las Cruces
Carlsbad Caverns N.P. ■

Tucson ●   □ Saguaro N.M.
□ Organ Pipe Cactus N.M.   Dragoon ●   TEXAS
Chiricahua N.M. □

●El Paso

SONORA   CHIHUAHUA

MEXICO

0   50   100   150   km

0   25   50   75   100   mi

Gulf of California   ●Casas Grandes

Dragoon	(southeast of Tucson) *The Amerind Foundation:* a modern building in typical Southwest architectural style; prehistoric and historic cultures; fine collection of pottery from Casas Grandes.
Flagstaff	*Museum of Northern Arizona* (north of the city): Large collection of prehistoric and historic objects.
Globe	*Gila Pueblo Archaeological Foundation* (founded by Harold S. Gladwin in 1927): Prehistoric cultures. *Clara T. Woody Museum of Gila County.* Salado Culture. Collection of artifacts from the Besh-ba-Gowah Ruins near Globe.
Grand Canyon National Park	Visitor center, museum, petroglyphs. Access to some areas is difficult. The 5,940-foot-deep canyon in the Colorado Plateau is considered to be one of the seven wonders of the world. *The Tusayan Museum* specializes in the culture of contemporary Pueblo Indians.
Homolovi	(west of Winslow) Petroglyphs, not easily accessible.
Honanki and Palatki	(southwest of Sedona) Pueblo ruins and petroglyphs, most of which are difficult to reach.
Montezuma Castle National Monument	Visitor center, museum. Sinagua Culture. The site was named by the first Spanish explorers, who attributed it to the Aztecs. A spectacular monument, a sort of unconquerable fortress, built on the top of the pale pink limestone cliffs above Beaver Creek, a tributary of the Verde River. The five-story "castle" has 20 rooms and was inhabited between 1100 and 1400. The only access, as is the case with many cliff dwellings, is by means of a series of ladders. Seven miles away is *Montezuma Well,* a naturally occurring, spring-fed, perfectly round limestone pool. It is 56 feet deep, with a diameter of 478 feet. Almost 2 million gallons of water flow into it daily, providing an oasis in the middle of a barren land. The Sinagua watered their fields with an intricate system of canals that are still in use today.
Monument Valley Navajo Tribal Park	Visitor center, museum. The monolithic, bizarre sandstone shapes are among the most remarkable natural phenomena in the United States.
Navajo National Monument	Visitor center, museum, petroglyphs. Anasazi Culture. The three large cliff dwellings, also called the "Three Cities of Kayenta," were built around 1250. *Keet Seel* ("broken pottery" in the Navajo language) consists of 160 rooms, of which 75 are virtually intact, and six *kivas,* all built in a large rock shelter 346 feet long and 50 feet deep; it is the largest cliff dwelling in Arizona. *Betatkin* (Navajo for "house at the edge of the abyss") several miles southeast of Keet Seel, is one of the most impressive cliff dwellings of the Southwest. Built in the middle of a 500-foot high sandstone cliff into an enormous 230-foot high rocky overhang, it contains 135 rooms in houses and towers several stories high, as well as six *kivas. Inscription House,* named after a 14th-century inscription that is unfortunately no longer legible, is 30 miles west of Keet Seel. The site has 75 rooms and one *kiva;* it is currently under restoration and not open to visitors.
Organ Pipe Cactus National Monument	(south of Ajo) Visitor center. Unique landscape with interesting desert plants and animals, named after the organ pipe cactus, which grows only in this spot.
Petrified Forest/ Painted Desert National Park	Visitor center, museum, petroglyphs. Access difficult in some areas. The petrified tree trunks found throughout the area are more than 200 million years old. A film at the visitor center describes the unique landscape of the Painted Desert.

Phoenix	Capital of Arizona, tourist information available at the Phoenix and Valley of the Sun Convention and Visitors Bureau. *The Heard Museum of Anthropology and Primitive Art* holds one of the most comprehensive collections of Southwest Indian artifacts, in particular a large collection of kachinas (Barry Goldwater Collection) and Navajo blankets. *Pueblo Grande Museum:* Visitor center, ruins adjacent to the museum. Hohokam Culture.
Saguaro National Monument	Visitor center, museum, petroglyphs. This 85,000-acre nature preserve, adjacent to the city of Tucson, is the home of the giant cactus, the saguaro, which can attain an age of 200 years and a height of 50 feet.
Snaketown	(27 miles south of Phoenix) Hohokam Culture. Will be called the Hohokam-Pima National Monument in a few years, not currently open to visitors. Snaketown, *skoaquik* in the Pima language, the "capital" of the Hohokam, was founded in 300 B.C. and was inhabited until 1100. In the course of centuries it grew to encompass an area of almost 400 acres, which included thousands of houses and other buildings. According to the calculations of Emil W. Haury, the foremost authority on Snaketown, a house was occupied for about 25 years. It was constructed of adobe-covered brush supported by posts. Every century approximately 400 new buildings were built, until they numbered about 5,000. The Hohokam also built many irrigation canals that were several miles long, allowing them to make optimal use of their fields. In addition, there were two ball courts in Snaketown. It is likely that this was the site of the largest Indian community in the Southwest.
Tonto National Monument	Visitor center, museum. Salado Culture. Impressive Salado village consisting of two pueblos with a total of 60 rooms built into the rock shelter of a steep cliff face. The dryness of the caves preserved remnants of cotton fabric that are among the most beautiful examples found in the Southwest.
Tucson	The *Arizona State Museum* (University of Arizona) houses a collection of beautiful artifacts from all Southwest cultures, particularly Hohokam artifacts. The *Arizona Sonora Desert Museum* (west of Tucson) exhibits flora and fauna of the Southwest and is one of the most intelligently conceived open-air museums in the world.
Tuzigoot National Monument	(east of Flagstaff) Visitor center, museum. Sinagua Culture. Located 23 miles northwest of *Montezuma Castle,* this ruin of 110 rooms is 528 feet long and 100 feet wide. It is situated on a hill with a panoramic view overlooking the Verde Valley. The village experienced two cultural peaks, the first around 1200 and the second after 1300.
Walnut Canyon National Monument	(east of Flagstaff) Visitor center, museum, petroglyphs. Sinagua Culture. There are more than 200 villages here, built between 1000 and 1250 on the mesas and cliffs of a narrow canyon, many located in small rock shelters. A large number of the approximately 300 rooms have the characteristic ventilation hole above the door. The many walnut trees growing at the bottom of the canyon not only lent it its name but also served as an important food source for the people who lived here.
Wupatki National Monument	Visitor center, museum, petroglyphs. Sinagua Culture. The eruption of the Sunset Crater, a natural catastrophe that occurred in the Flagstaff area in 1064–1065, had great significance for the development of the Sinagua. On the one hand it brought death and destruction, covering 4,800 square miles with lava and ash and forcing all survivors to flee. On the other hand, soon after the catastrophe the ash dispersed and a thin sheet of hardened material

remained, providing the soil with a protective layer that considerably reduced evaporation. Once-barren fields became fertile. The returning Sinagua soon realized the effects of Sunset Crater and their civilization reached its height between 1087 and 1250. One of their finest achievements was the *wupatki* (the name is a Hopi word meaning "big house"). Built of large sandstone blocks, the pueblo rises in what is today arid country. There are about 100 houses as high as three stories, which were inhabited from 1100 until 1220. There are also an amphitheater and a ball court.

COLORADO

Boulder

University of Colorado Museum: Magnificent pottery collection of all Southwest cultures.

Denver

Capital of Colorado, tourist information available at the Denver Metro Convention and Visitors Bureau. *Colorado State Museum; Museum of Natural History; Historical Society of Colorado.*

Hovenweep National Monument

(Colorado and Utah) Visitor center, museum, petroglyphs. Anasazi Culture. Thirty miles west of Mesa Verde lie the ruins of six pueblos with an astonishing number of towers (more than 80). It is estimated that they were built between 1100 and 1300. The most impressive and best-preserved site is *Square Tower Ruins.* Access to the others is difficult. Architecturally and in terms of their geographic location they offer an unusual sight: Were they really built by the Anasazi? *Hovenweep* is a Ute Indian word meaning "abandoned valley."

Mesa Verde National Park

Visitor center, museum and bookstore near *Spruce Tree House,* petroglyphs. Anasazi Culture. The name "green table" comes from the evergreen pine forests and juniper thickets that cover most of the mesa. In the 52,695 acres of the park alone there are more than 5,000 ruins representing a variety of building styles. The oldest site goes back to the seventh century. Mesa Verde reached its cultural high point in the 12th and 13th centuries. The climatic conditions are ideal: There is a long frost-free period (160–170 days), the summer temperatures are bearable and there is a regular period of rainfall from July to August. The tops of the mesas were covered with a layer of fertile soil. *Cliff Palace* (1073–1272), with 200 small rooms, 23 *kivas,* and buildings as high as three stories, is the largest and best-known cliff dwelling in America. The Anasazi built it in a huge rock shelter 330 feet long, 100 feet wide and 66 feet high. Fourteen "mummies" were discovered in one of the rooms. The other significant cliff dwellings at Mesa Verde are *Square Tower House* (not an isolated tower originally; the other buildings have collapsed), one of the most impressive ruins, with 80 rooms; *Balcony House,* consisting of 45 rooms, two *kivas* and, a rare occurrence, a spring; *Juniper House,* with 31 rooms and three *kivas; Spruce Tree House,* named in 1891 by Richard Wetherill, who discovered it, after a more than 200-year-old spruce nearby, with 114 rooms and eight *kivas* in a 1980-foot-long and 90-foot-deep rock shelter; *Wetherill Mesa,* the site of *Long House,* with 150 rooms and 21 *kivas,* the largest cliff dwelling after Cliff Palace; and *Step House* and *Mug House,* where more than 400 mugs, pots and jars were found.

NEW MEXICO

Abiquiu

The Florence Hawley Ellis Museum of Anthropology, Ghost Ranch: Prehistoric and historic. Indian cultures.

Albuquerque

Tourist information available at the Albuquerque Convention and Visitors Bureau. *Maxwell Museum of Anthropology:* Large collection of prehistoric and early historic finds in the Southwest. *Indian Pueblo Cultural Center:* A cultural center, museum and activity center dedicated to the preservation of Pueblo culture, the floor plan is based on the D-shape of Pueblo Bonito, and high-quality crafts are sold here. *Indian Petroglyph State Park.* Several miles outside of Albuquerque, petroglyphs, readily accessible.

Aztec Ruins National Monument

Visitor center, museum. Anasazi Culture. Large Anasazi pueblo located between Chaco Canyon and Mesa Verde. Aztec consists of 500 rooms laid out in an E-shaped plan around a plaza. There are also 23 small *kivas* and a great *kiva* with a diameter of 40 feet that was restored in 1934. The basic plan is a rectangle measuring 360148280 feet and the buildings are as much as three stories and 30 feet high. The town was built within 1,650 feet of the Animas River, a tributary of the San Juan River. Aztec had a population of approximately 450 during its two cultural flowerings, from 1110 to 1124 and from 1220 to 1280. The site was named in the 19th century by early American settlers who thought the pueblo had been built by the Aztecs.

Bandelier National Monument

Visitor center, petroglyphs (the famous *Painted Cave*). Anasazi Culture. Named after the archaeologist Adolph Bandelier, this federal reserve in Frijoles Canyon has some impressive cliff dwellings sheltered in the volcanic rock of the Pajarito Plateau. *Long House* is an example, with 300 rooms and a length of 825 feet (the source of its name). *Tyuonyi,* the main Anasazi town, was built on the valley floor, while other ruins (*Tsankawi, Otowi, Tseregi*) are located on top of the mesa. Tyuonyi, inhabited from 1100–1550, is an oval village, built around a central plaza, with a single narrow entrance. There are 400 small rooms and three large *kivas* built out of blocks of volcanic rock. The houses are two stories high, with terraced roofs. Bandelier found two unusual features: The *kivas,* one with a diameter of 20 feet, were chipped out of the rock they are built on, the only example of their kind in the Southwest, and there are two stone "jaguars," weathered life-size animal shapes that were carved out of the rock of the cliff centuries ago. They are located at the top of the mesa, 9 miles from the visitor center; several miles south are two more figures. These two pairs are unique in the Southwest.

Carlsbad Caverns National Park

Visitor center. One of the largest caverns in the world (47,302 acres), whose deepest cave lies 1,039 feet under the surface. In the summer the caves are home to about 250,000 bats that winter in Mexico.

Chaco Culture National Historical Park

Visitor center, museum, petroglyphs (painting of the "super nova"), some readily accessible. Anasazi Culture. In this canyon, 17 miles long and 1 mile across, bordered by cliff faces rising 330 feet, are 2,000 ruins; among them are 13 pueblos and one great *kiva* dating from the eighth century. According to the most recent calculations, the maximum Chaco Canyon population from the 11th to the 13th century was around 2,000, not the 4,000 or more that had previously been assumed. Among the most significant sites, each with five to 35 *kivas,* are *Una Vida* (100 rooms), *Hungo Pavi* (150 rooms), *Chetro Ketl* (500 rooms), *Tsin Kletsin*

(155 rooms), *Kin Kletso* (135 rooms), *Pueblo del Arroyo* (285 rooms), *Pueblo Alto* (120 rooms), *Casa Chiquita* (80 rooms), *Penasco Blanco* (215 rooms), and the two architectural jewels, *Pueblo Bonito* and the *kiva* of *Casa Rinconanda*.

Pueblo Bonito (the beautiful village), built between 920 and 1130, was created according to a preconceived plan; the perfectly constructed buildings, two to four stories high, form a semicircle with a 538-foot base, divided into two sections by a wall. The pueblo consisted of 800 rooms, 35 *kivas* with an average diameter of 26 feet and two great *kivas* with diameters measuring 60 and 40 feet respectively. The rooms are about 8 feet high and in general larger than those of other pueblos. Those on the ground floor (56 feet square) are connected—sometimes as many as 20 or 30, as in the case of Chetro Ketl—through a line of T-shaped or rectangular doors, producing a spectacular visual effect. Today it is assumed that these were not family dwellings, but instead were used for religious ceremonies. This accounts for the revision of population figures; it is now believed that around 1130, only 100 to 200 people lived at this site. Whatever the case, Neil M. Judd, who excavated a large portion of the ruin, believed the pueblo to have been the largest "apartment house" in the New World before a larger one was constructed in New York in 1882. For a long time, even during the golden age of Chaco, Pueblo Bonito existed under the threat of an enormous overhanging rock. On January 22, 1942, *Threatening Rock* did fall on the northeast part of the pueblo, destroying 30 rooms.

The *kiva* of *Casa Rinconada,* built around 1100, forms a perfect circle with a diameter of 62 feet, hence its name meaning "without corners." Between 1000 and 1100 Chaco Canyon was undoubtedly an important center for Anasazi Culture. A complex of streets and paths linked several communities in a circumference of several hundred miles. It is thought that cooperatives were formed for the cultivation of the fields and the manufacture of utilitarian and ceremonial objects.

Coronado State Monument	Visitor center, museum (frescoes of Kuaua). The site is named in honor of the first Spanish expedition into the Southwest (1540–1542), led by Francisco Vásquez de Coronado. The restored *kiva* contains copies of magnificent 15th-century frescoes; the originals are stored in the nearby museum.
El Morro National Monument	Visitor center, prehistoric petroglyphs. The main attraction is *Inscription Rock,* a 2,756-foot-high sandstone rock face with hundreds of inscriptions made by Spanish explorers and American pioneers from the 17th to the 19th century.
Galisteo	There are many beautiful petroglyphs in the area.
Gallup	*Museum of Indian Arts and Crafts:* Several centuries of Indian crafts from various cultures.
Gila Cliff Dwellings National Monument	Visitor center, museum, petroglyphs. Mogollon Culture. This village is situated on a tributary of the Gila River in the Mogollon Mountains, which were already inhabited in 400 B.C. The cliff dwellings, approximately 40 well-constructed rooms built under a rock shelter below the top of the mesa, were built between 1250 and 1300. Adolph Bandelier was the first archaeologist to examine the ruins.
Las Cruces	*New Mexico State University Museum:* Collection of Mogollon and Casas Grandes pottery (artifacts from local excavations).

Pecos National Monument	Visitor center, museum. Anasazi Culture. Between 1300 and the middle of the 14th century, *Pecos Pueblo,* located in a fertile valley with water supplied by the Pecos River, played a decisive role in the exploration, colonization and conversion to Catholicism of the people of New Mexico. It was one of the largest and easternmost pueblos reached by the conquistadors. From 1300 until 1838 the pueblo, up to four stories and encompassing 1,100 rooms, had a population of approximately 2,500 Indian people. As a consequence of its favorable location between the Great Plains, inhabited by nomadic buffalo hunters, and the sedentary farmers of the Rio Grande Valley, it assumed a key position as a commercial center in the eastern Southwest. Pecos has been well documented, especially by Alfred Kidder.
Portales	*Blackwater Draw Museum:* Artifacts from the Paleo-Indian and Archaic Periods of the Southwest. *Miles Museum and Paleo-Indian Institute:* Introduces the visitor to the time of early human habitation of the Southwest.
Puye Cliff Dwellings	A cliff dwelling constructed in the soft volcanic rock of *Santa Clara Canyon* (Santa Clara Reservation).
Salinas National Monument	*Gran Quivira National Monument:* Visitor center, museum, ruins of a 17th-century Spanish mission. *Abo State Monument:* Visitor center, museum, ruins of a mission church built of red sandstone in 1630. *Quarai State Monument:* Visitor center, museum, ruin of a 17th-century Spanish church. These three ruins are good examples of the transition from the prehistoric to the historic periods.
Sandia Man Cave National Historic Landmark	Cave in the Sandia Mountains in which the earliest traces of Southwest Indians were found. (This site is reached by means of a metal scaffold.)
Santa Fe	Tourist information available at the Santa Fe Convention and Visitors Bureau. *Laboratory of Anthropology:* Large collection of Southwest Indian artifacts. *Palace of the Governors:* The oldest public building in the United States (1610), prehistoric and early historic collection. International Folk Art Foundation (founded in 1953): A unique museum with a folk-art collection of over 120,000 pieces (clothing, toys, textiles, etc.) from more than 50 countries. *Institute of American Indian Arts Museum:* Contemporary Indian art. *Wheelwright Museum* (formerly The Museum of Navajo Ceremonial Art): Inside this museum, which is built in the shape of a Navajo hogan, are more than 600 reproductions of Navajo sand paintings, and pieces drafted in silver, baskets, blankets and other cultural items are displayed. Tapes play Indian songs and there is a library. *The Museum of Indian Arts and Culture:* Exhibits of prehistoric and early historic Indian cultures in Arizona and New Mexico.
Taos	Tourist information is available at the Tourist Information Desk of the Taos Chamber of Commerce and a mission church, museum and gallery are in town. The famous *Taos Pueblo* is located in Ranchos de Taos. It includes two five-story housing complexes built in the traditional style, which are inhabited and are accessible only by ladder. Taos was built 600 years ago at a time when Indians left the San Juan Valley due to drought; the fact that the pueblo has been preserved unchanged to the present day in spite of tourism is due to the efforts of the residents. *Millicent Rogers Museum:* A private collection of modern Indian art and crafts and Spanish religious art that is open to the public.

Three Rivers Petroglyph Site	(30 miles north of Alamogordo) Petroglyphs, including over 5,000 representations of human figures, animals and abstract shapes. Easy access.
White Sands National Monument	Visitor center, high dunes of pure white gypsum.

UTAH

Anasazi Indian Village State Historical Monument	Visitor center, museum. The most important Anasazi finds north of the Colorado River were discovered here. The Anasazi village is a reconstruction.
Arches National Park	Visitor center, museum, petroglyphs. Some areas are easily accessible. Two hundred natural bridges and arches of red sandstone, the products of erosion, are found here. Among the best known are *Delicate Arch* and *Landscape Arch,* the latter spanning a distance of 293 feet.
Bryce Canyon National Park	Visitor center, museum. Named after the first settler, Ebenezer Bryce, this is without a doubt one of the most beautiful natural preserves in the world, a fantastically eroded landscape with bizarre sandstone formations in all imaginable shades of red, violet, pink, ochre, yellow and white. The Paiute gave the area the appropriate name of "Red Rocks, Standing Like Men in a Bowl-Shaped Canyon."
Canyonlands National Park	Visitor center, petroglyphs. These impassive canyons at the confluence of the Colorado and Green Rivers are the site of numerous pictographs, like those found in *Horse* and *Horseshoe Canyons,* at *Peek-aboo Spring* and in *Salt Creek Canyon.* Particularly worth seeing are the several yards-long friezes of human figures that decorate the walls of Horseshoe Canyon, and the "All American Man" at Salt Creek Canyon, a figure painted red, white and blue.
Capitol Reef National Park	Visitor center, museum, petroglyphs, some readily accessible. This approximately 96-mile-long park, which borders on Glen Canyon National Recreation Area to the south, is characterized by a diversity of landscapes, sandstone formations and narrow canyons and gorges. Worth seeing are the petroglyphs in *Capitol Gorge, Cathedral Valley* and the *Fremont River Gorge.*
Cedar Breaks National Monument	Visitor center. A miniature version of Bryce Canyon, with fantastic rock formations and a large, natural amphitheater.
Central Utah Area	Numerous pictographs can be found in Sheep Canyon, Bullard Cove, Black Dragon Canyon, Nine Mile Canyon, Hog Springs, Price River Gorge, Cottonwood Canyon, Rochester Creek and in other places in this area.
Dinosaur National Monument	(Utah and Colorado) Visitor center, museum, petroglyphs. Access is difficult. Significant dinosaur remains have been found. Some of the fossils can be viewed at the site.

Glen Canyon National Recreation Area — Visitor center, museum. Recreation area surrounding Lake Powell, a very large reservoir on the Colorado created by the enormous Glen Canyon Dam. *Rainbow Bridge National Monument:* One of the largest and most beautiful natural bridges in the world, with petroglyphs. Access is difficult.

Grand Gulch Primitive Area — Petroglyphs in *Bullet Canyon* and in *Main Canyon.*

Indian Creek State Park — Petroglyphs. Best known is *Newspaper Rock State Historical Monument* (readily accessible), a smooth rock wall with 350 inscriptions reminiscent of a newspaper; one of the oldest "entries" is said to have originated in the 12th century or earlier. Other petroglyphs in the area are more difficult to reach.

Moab — There are many petroglyphs in the area around this small town, in Mill Creek Canyon, Cane Creek Canyon, Behind the Rocks, Colorado River Gorge, Spanish Valley, etc. Many are not easily accessible.

Natural Bridges National Monument — Visitor center, museum, petroglyphs. Three spectacular rock bridges created by wind and water erosion; cliff dwellings from the early historical period.

Price — *College of Eastern Utah Prehistoric Museum.* Fremont Culture.

Provo — *Museum of Archaeology and Ethnology.* Fremont Culture.

San Juan River Gorge — Petroglyphs *(Butler Wash, Sand Island).* Access is sometimes difficult.

San Raphael Swell — Petroglyphs. *Temple Mountain Wash* and *Buckhorn Wash* are readily accessible; other sites are more difficult to reach.

Vernal — *Utah Field House of Natural History.* Basketmaker and Fremont Cultures.

Zion National Park — Visitor center, museum, petroglyphs. A marvelous landscape of canyons up to 35,000 feet deep and narrow gorges, the so-called narrows, sometimes only a few feet wide.

The following museums also have important collections of Southwest Indian art and artifacts:

New York — *Museum of the American Indian, Heye Foundation; American Museum of Natural History*
Washington, D.C. — *National Museum of Natural History, Smithsonian Institution*
Cambridge, Mass. — *Peabody Museum of American Archaeology and Ethnology, Harvard University*
Andover, Mass. — *Phillips Academy*
Chicago, Ill. — *Field Museum of Natural History*
Los Angeles, Calif. — *The Southwest Museum*
Salt Lake City, Utah — *Museum of Natural History*

BIBLIOGRAPHY

The following titles represent only a selection of the most important works about the Southwest.

General Works

Amsden, Charles A.: *Prehistoric Southwesterners from Basketmaker to Pueblo*. Southwest Museum, Los Angeles, 1949 (reprinted 1976).

Bandelier, Adolph F.: *Final Report of Investigations Among the Indians of the Southwestern United States, Carried on Mainly in the Years from 1880 to 1885*. 2 vols. (Paper of the Archaeological Institute of America, American Series 3 and 4), Harvard University Press, Cambridge, Mass., 1890–1892.

Barnes, F.A.: *Canyon Country Prehistoric Rock Art*. Wasatch Publishers, Salt Lake City, 1982.

Barnett, Franklin: *Dictionary of Prehistoric Indian Artifacts of the American Southwest*. Northland Press, Flagstaff, 1973.

Cassells, E. Steve: *The Archaeology of Colorado*. Johnson Books, Boulder, 1983.

Ceram, C.W.: *The First American*. Harcourt Brace Jovanovich, New York, 1971.

Cordell, Linda S.: *Prehistory of the Southwest*. Academic Press, New York, 1984.

Early Man in America. Readings from *Scientific American*. Freeman, San Francisco, 1972.

Horgan, Paul: *The Heroic Triad. Essays in the Social Energies of Three Southwestern Cultures*. Holt, Rinehart and Winston, New York, 1970.

Jennings, Jesse D., ed: *Ancient North Americans*. Freeman, San Francisco, 1978, 1983.

Josephy Jr., Alvin M.: *The Indian Heritage of America*. Bantam Books, New York, 1978.

Kidder, Alfred Vincent and Irving Rouse: *An Introduction to the Study of Southwestern Archaeology, with a Preliminary Account of the Excavations at Pecos, with a Summary of Southwestern Archaeology Today*. Yale University Press, New Haven, 1962.

Lange, Frederick W. and Diana Leonard: *Among Ancient Ruins. The Legacy of Earl H. Morris*. Johnson Books, Boulder, 1985.

Lister, Florence C. and Robert H.: *Earl Morris and Southwestern Archaeology*. University of New Mexico Press, Albuquerque, 1968.
———: *Those who Came Before*. University of Arizona Press, Tucson, 1983.

Martin, Paul S. and Fred Plog: *The Archaeology of Arizona*. Doubleday Natural History Press, Garden City, 1973.

McGregor, John C.: *Southwestern Archaeology*. University of Illinois Press, Urbana, 1965.

Noble, David G.: *Ancient Ruins of the Southwest*. Northland Press, Flagstaff, 1981.

Ortiz, Alfonso A., ed: *Handbook of North American Indians, Vol. 9: Southwest*. Smithsonian Institution, Washington, D.C., 1979.

Tanner, Clara Lee: *Prehistoric Southwestern Craft Arts*. University of Arizona Press, Tucson, 1976.

Wills, W.H.: *Early Prehistoric Agriculture in the American Southwest*. School of American Research Press, Santa Fe, 1988.

Wissler, Clark: *Indians of the United States*. Doubleday & Company, New York, 1966.

The World of the American Indian. National Geographic Society, Washington, D.C., 1974.

Wormington, H. Marie: *Prehistoric Indians of the Southwest*. The Denver Museum of Natural History, Popular Series, No. 7, Denver, 1947.

Dendrochronology

Stallings Jr., W.S.: *Dating Prehistoric Ruins by Tree-Rings*. University of Arizona Press, Tucson, 1939 (rev. ed 1960).

Stokes, Marvon A. and Terah L. Smiley: *An Introduction to Tree-Ring Dating*. University of Chicago Press, Chicago, 1968.

Religion, Myths, Symbols

Bandelier, Adolph F.: *The Delight Makers*. Dodd, Mead and Co., New York, 1918 (reprint 1971).

Packard, Gary and Maggy: *Suns and Serpents. The Symbolism of Indian Rock Art*. Packard Publications, Santa Fe, 1974.

Tyler, Hamilton A.: *Pueblo, Gods and Myths*. University of Oklahoma Press, Norman, 1964.

Waters, Frank: *Masked Gods: Navaho and Pueblo Symbolism*. Sage Books, The Swallow Press, Chicago, 1950.
———: *Book of the Hopi*. Ballentine Books, New York, 1972.

The Hohokam Culture

Doyel, David and Fred Plog (eds): *Current Issues in Hohokam Prehistory*. Arizona State University, Anthropological Research Papers No. 23, Tempe, 1980.

Haury, Emil W.: *The Hohokam: Desert Farmers and Craftsmen. Excavations at Snaketown, 1964–1965*. University of Arizona Press, Tucson, 1976.

Wilcox, David R. and Lynette O. Shenk: *The Architecture of the Casa Grande and its Interpretation*. Archaeological Series No. 115, Arizona State Museum, Tucson, 1977.

The Mogollan and Mimbres Cultures

Brody, J.J.: *Mimbres Painted Pottery*. University of New Mexico Press, Albuquerque, 1977.

Cosgrove, H.S. and C.B.: *The Swarts Ruin: A Typical Mimbres Site in Southwestern New Mexico*. Papers of the Peabody Museum of American Archaeology and Ethnology (Harvard University) 15, Cambridge, Mass., 1932.

Haury, Emil W.: *Mogollon Culture in the Forestdale Valley, East-Central Arizona*. University of Arizona Press, Tucson, 1985.

LeBlanc, Steven A.: *The Mimbres People*. Thames and Hudson, London, 1983.

Wheat, Joe B.: *Mogollon Culture Prior to A.D. 1000*. American Anthropological Association, Memoir No. 82, Menasha, 1955.

The Anasazi Culture

Ambler, Richard J.: *The Anasazi*. Museum of Northern Arizona, Flagstaff, 1977.

Anderson, Douglas and Barbara: *Chaco Canyon, Center of a Culture*. Southwest Parks and Monuments Association, Globe, 1981.

Breternitz, David A. and Jack E. Smith: *Mesa Verde and Rocky Mountains National Parks. National Parkways*. Vol. III–IV, National Parks Division of World-Wide Research and Publishing Co., Casper, WY, 1972.

Corbett, John M.: *Aztec Ruins*. National Park Service, Washington, D.C., 1962.

Grant, Campbell: *Canyon de Chelly. Its People and Rock Art*. University of Arizona Press, Tucson, 1978.

Hayes, Alden C.: *The Archaeological Survey of Wetherill Mesa, Mesa Verde National Park, Colorado*. Archaeological Research Series No. 7-A, National Park Service, Washington, D.C., 1964.

Howard, Richard M.: *The Mesa Verde Museum*. Mesa Verde Museum Association, Mesa Verde National Park, 1968.

Judd, Neil M.: *The Architecture of Pueblo Bonito*. Smithsonian Miscellaneous Collections Vol. 147, Washington, D.C. 1964.

Judge, W. James and John D. Schelberg, eds: *Recent Research on Chaco Prehistory*. Reports of the Chaco Center No. 8, Albuquerque, 1984.

Kidder, Alfred V.: *Pecos, New Mexico*. Papers of the Robert S. Peabody Foundation for Archaeology 5, Andover, Mass., 1958.

Lekson, Stephen H.: *Great Pueblo Architecture of Chaco Canyon, New Mexico*. University of New Mexico Press, Albuquerque, 1986.

Lister, Robert H. and Florence C.: *Chaco Canyon, Archaeology and Archaeologists*. University of New Mexico Press, Albuquerque, 1981.

Longacre, William A., ed: *Restructuring Prehistoric Pueblo Societies*. University of New Mexico Press, Albuquerque, 1970.

Noble, David G.: *New Light on Chaco Canyon*. School of American Research Press, Santa Fe, 1984.

Nordenskiöld, Gustaf E.A.: *The Cliff Dwellers of the Mesa Verde, Southwestern Colorado*. New York, 1973 (first published Stockholm, 1893).

Reyman, Jonathan E.: *Astronomy, Architecture, and Adaptation at Puebo Bonito. Science*, Vol. 193, 1976.

Rohn, Arthur H.: *Mug House, Mesa Verde National Park*. Archaeological Research Series No. 7-D, National Park Service, Washington, D.C., 1971.

Supplee, Charles and Douglas and Barbara Anderson: *Canyon de Chelly, The Story Behind the Scenery*. KC Publications, Las Vegas, 1971.

Vivian, R. Gordon and Paul Reiter: *The Great Kivas of Chaco Canyon and Their Relationships*. Monographs of the School of American Research 22, Santa Fe, 1960.

Vivian, R. Gwinn, Dulce N. Dodgen, and Gayle H. Hartmann: *Wooden Ritual Artifacts from Chaco Canyon, New Mexico. The Chetro Ketl Collection*. The University of Arizona Press, Tucson, 1978.

Watson, Don: *Cliff Dwellings of the Mesa Verde*. Mesa Verde Museum Association, Mesa Verde National Park, 1961.

Wenger, Gilbert R.: *The Story of Mesa Verde National Park*. Mesa Verde Museum Association, Mesa Verde National Park, 1980.

The Sinagua Culture

Colton, Harold S.: *The Sinagua: A Summary of the Archaeology of the Region of Flagstaff, Arizona*. Museum of Northern Arizona, Bulletin 22, Flagstaff, 1946.

Schroeder, Albert H. and Homer F. Hastings: *Montezuma Castle*. National Park Service, Washington, D.C., 1985.

Van Valkenburgh, Sallie P.: *Archaeological Site Survey at Walnut Canyon National Park. Plateau*, 34, Flagstaff, 1961.

The Fremont Culture

Marwitt, John P.: *Fremont Cultures. Handbook of North American Indian. Vol. 11: Great Basin*. Washington, D.C., 1986.

Wormington, H. Marie: *A Reappraisal of the Fremont Culture*. Denver Museum of Natural History, Denver, 1955.

Casas Grandes

Di Peso, Charles C.: *Casas Grandes: A Fallen Trading Center of the Grand Chichimeca*. 3 vols. Northland Press, Flagstaff, 1974.

Pottery

Amsden, Charles A.: *An Analysis of Hohokam Pottery Design*. Medallion Papers 23, Globe, 1936.

Arnold, David L.: "Pueblo Pottery. 200 Years of Artistry." *National Geographic*, 162, Washington, D.C., November, 1982.

Breternitz, David A., Arthur H. Rohn and A. Morris: *Prehistoric Ceramics of the Mesa Verde Region*. Museum of Northern Arizona, Ceramic Services, No. 5, Flagstaff, 1974.

Brody, J.J., Catherine J. Scott and Steven A. LeBlanc: *Mimbres Pottery*, Hudson Hills Press, New York, 1983.

Carr, Pat: *Mimbres Mythology*. Southwestern Studies, No. 56, University of Texas, El Paso, 1979.

Colton, Harold S. and Lyndon L. Hargrave: *Handbook of Northern Arizona Pottery Wares*. Museum of Northern Arizona Bulletin 11, Flagstaff, 1937.

Fewkes, J. Walter: *Designs on Prehistoric Hopi Pottery*. Smithsonian Institution, 33rd Annual Report of the Bureau of American Ethnology, Washington, D.C., 1919 (reprinted Dover Publications, New York, 1973).

Kabotie, Fred: *Designs from the Ancient Mimbreños with a Hopi Interpretation*. Northland Press, Flagstaff, 1982.

Wormington, H. Marie and Arminta Neal: *The Story of Pueblo Pottery*. Denver Museum of Natural History, Museum Pictorial No. 2, Denver, 1951, 1965.

Kivas

Dutton, Bertha P.: *Sun Father's Way: The Kiva Murals of Kuaua*. University of New Mexico Press, Albuquerque, 1963.

Smith, Watson: *Kiva Mural Decorations at Awatovi and Kawaika-a, with a Survey of Other Wall Paintings in the Pueblo Southwest*. Papers of the Peabody Museum of American Archaeology and Ethnology 37, Cambridge, Mass., 1952.

Petroglyphs

Barnes, F.A.: *Canyon Country Prehistoric Rock Art*. Wasatch Publishers, Salt Lake City, 1982.

Castleton, Kenneth B.: *Petroglyphs and Pictographs of Utah*. 2 vols., Utah Museum of Natural History, Salt Lake City, 1978.

Grant, Campbell: *Rock Art of the American Indian*. Crowell, New York, 1967 (Apollo Edition, 1972).

Grant, Campbell: *The Rock Art of the North American Indians*. Cambridge University Press, Cambridge, 1983.

Mallery, Garrick: *Picture-Writing of the American Indians*. Smithsonian Institution, 10th Annual Report of the Bureau of American Ethnology, Washington, D.C., 1983 (reprinted Dover, New York, 1972).

Martineau, LaVan: *The Rocks Begin to Speak*. KC Publications, Las Vegas, 1973.

Schaafsma, Polly: *The Rock Art of Utah*. Papers of the Peabody Museum of Archaeology and Ethnology 65, Cambridge, Mass., 1971.

———: *Rock Art in New Mexico*. University of New Mexico Press, Albuquerque, 1975.

———: *Indian Rock Art of the Southwest*. University of New Mexico Press, Albuquerque, 1980.

Weaver Jr., Donald E.: *Images on Stone. The Prehistoric Rock Art of the Colorado Plateau*. The Museum of Northern Arizona, Flagstaff, 1984.

The Historic Period

Dozier, Edward P.: *The Pueblo Indians of North America*. Holt, Rinehart and Winston, New York, 1970.

Frank, Lawrence P. and Francis H. Harlow: *Historic Pottery of the Pueblo Indians, 1600–1800*. New York Graphic Society, New York, 1974.

Harlow, Francis H.: *Modern Pueblo Pottery, 1880–1960*. Flagstaff, 1977.

Ortiz, Alfonso: *The Tewa World: Space, Time, Being, and Becoming in a Pueblo Society*. Chicago University Press, Chicago, 1969.

Ortiz, Alfonso (ed): *New Perspectives on the Pueblos*. University of New Mexico Press, Albuquerque, 1972.

Talayesva, Don C.: *Sun Chief: The Autobiography of a Hopi Indian*. Edited by Leo W. Simmons. Yale University Press, New Haven, 1942.

INDEX

ACKNOWLEDGMENTS

The authors thank the following persons and institutions for the spontaneous and generous help received when they were gathering material for this book. Thanks also to those authors whose books are mentioned and quoted in the text; their works relevant to this book are listed in the bibliography.

Garth Bawden, Director, Maxwell Museum of Anthropology, University of New Mexico, Albuquerque

Allen Bohnert, Museum Curator, Mesa Verde National Park (Colorado)

Robert A. Coody, Assistant Conservator, Museum of Northern Arizona, Flagstaff

Thomas B. Carrol, Superintendent, Salinas National Monument (New Mexico)

Dabney Ford, Archaeologist, Chaco Culture National Hitorical Park (New Mexico)

Nancy Fox, Curator-Anthropology, Laboratory of Anthropology, Museum of New Mexico, Santa Fe

Robert C. Heyder, Superintendent, Mesa Verde National Park (Colorado)

Rowina Ellaine Hughes, Anthropology Collections Supervisor, Museum of Northern Arizona, Flagstaff

G. Michael Jacobs, Archaeological Collections Curator, Arizona State Museum, University of Arizona, Tucson

Frederick W. Lange, Curator of Anthropology, Museum, University of Colorado, Boulder

Diana Leonard, Assistant Curator of Anthropology, Museum, University of Colorado, Boulder

Rosalee A. Lucero, Researcher, All Indian Pueblo Council, Archives and Resource Center, Albuquerque

Allan J. McIntyre, Conservator, The Amerind Foundation, Dragoon (Arizona)

Ann E. Marshall, Curator of Collections, The Heard Museum, Phoenix (Arizona)

Virginia Robicheau, Museum Curator, Bandelier National Monument (New Mexico)

Marian, Rodee, Curator of Collections, Maxwell Museum of Anthropology, University of New Mexico, Albuquerque

Susie Schofield, Quarai, Salinas National Monument (New Mexico)

Jack E. Smith, Chief Park Archaeologist, Mesa Verde National Park (Colorado)

Helga Teiwes, Photographer, Arizona State Museum, University of Arizona, Tucson

Larry Thornton, Ranger, Gila Cliff Dwellings National Monument (New Mexico)

Donald E. Weaver Jr., Curator-Chief Archaeologist, Department of Anthropology, Museum of Northern Arizona, Flagstaff

Anne I. Woosley, Director, The Amerind Foundation, Dragoon (Arizona)

The authors especially wish to thank:

The National Park Service, Washington, D.C.

Professor Dr. Wolfgang Lindig, Institute for Historic Ethnology at the Johann-Wolfgang-Goethe-University, Frankfurt, for his careful technical reading of the text and his many valuable suggestions and encouragement.

Marianne Widmer, U. Bär Verlag

Alina Acatos for the innumerable hours spent on the final draft of the manuscript.

Eva Bruggmann for her help in procuring pictures during our trips to the Southwest.

Abbreviations

The abbreviations used in the captions represent the following museums:

AFM   Amerind Foundation Museum, Dragoon (Arizona)

ASM   Arizona State Museum, University of Arizona, Tucson

CCP   Museum Chaco Culture National Historical Park, Chaco Canyon (New Mexico)

HMP   Heard Museum, Phoenix (Arizona)

MMA   Maxwell Museum of Anthropology, University of New Mexico, Albuquerque

MNA   Museum of Northern Arizona, Flagstaff

MNM   Collections of the Museum of New Mexico, Laboratory of Anthropology, Santa Fe

MVM   Mesa Verde National Park Museum (Colorado)

SAR   School of American Research Collections in the Museum of New Mexico, Laboratory of Anthropology, Santa Fe

UCM   University of Colorado Museum, Boulder